DOUBLE CROSSING

Eva Salzman grew up in Brooklyn and on Long Island where she worked as a dancer/choreographer. At Stuyvesant High School her teacher was Frank McCourt; later, at Bennington College and Columbia University, where she received her MFA, she studied with Derek Walcott, Joseph Brodsky, C.K. Williams, Edmund White, Stanley Kunitz, Carolyn Kizer, Stephen Sandy, Elizabeth Hardwick and Jorie Graham. She moved to Britain in 1985 and lives in London.

Her teaching experience, for adults and children, has included projects in London's East End, a residency at Springhill Prison, continuing work for the Poetry Society's educational programmes, and co-devising a Start Writing Poetry course for the Open University. She has been Adjunct Professor at Friends World Programme (Long Island University – London), West Midlands Writing Fellow at Warwick University, where she co-taught the Poetry MA, and Royal Literary Fund Fellow at Ruskin College, Oxford.

Her grandmother was a child vaudeville actress; her mother is an environmentalist and her father a composer. This background, and a diverse range of jobs – Exercise Director of a Brooklyn orthodox Jewish diet centre, out-of-print book searcher and cleaner of rich ladies' houses – all inform her writing, especially her cross-arts projects with visual artists and performers. She has collaborated with director Rufus Norris and with composers Ian McQueen, Gary Carpenter, Rachel Leach, Philip Cashian, A.L. Nicolson, and her father, Eric Salzman. Her operas have been performed by the English National Opera Studio and abroad, in Olso, Vienna and Düsseldorf. She is currently writing an original libretto for Buxton Festival 2005. She has received grants from the Arts Council and Society of Authors, and won a Cholmondeley Award in 2004.

All her books have been Poetry Book Society Recommendations or Special Commendations. As well as new work, *Double Crossing* includes poems drawn from *The English Earthquake* (Bloodaxe Books, 1992), *Bargain with the Watchman* (Oxford University Press, 1997), the pamphlet *One Two* (Jones Press, 2002) and the fuller-length *One Two II* (Wrecking Ball Press, 2003).

EVA SALZMAN

DOUBLE CROSSING

NEW & SELECTED POEMS

To Benenden,
After a delightful visit with
delightful - and cheeky - girls,

[signature]

Writer in Residence
Jan/Feb. 2005

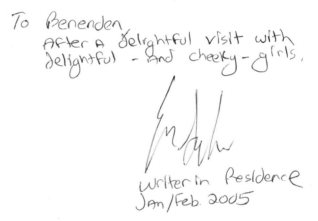

BLOODAXE BOOKS

ISBN: 1 85224 661 8

First published 2004 by
Bloodaxe Books Ltd,
Highgreen,
Tarset,
Northumberland NE48 1RP.

www.bloodaxebooks.com
For further information about Bloodaxe titles
please visit our website or write to
the above address for a catalogue.

Bloodaxe Books Ltd acknowledges
the financial assistance of
Arts Council England, North East.

Cover printing by J. Thomson Colour Printers Ltd, Glasgow.

Printed in Great Britain by
Cromwell Press Ltd, Trowbridge, Wiltshire.

*One must wait until evening to see
how splendid the day has been.*

SOPHOCLES

ACKNOWLEDGEMENTS

Double Crossing includes new work and poems drawn from *The English Earthquake* (Bloodaxe Books, 1992), *Bargain with the Watchman* (Oxford University Press, 1997), *One Two* (Jones Press 2002) and *One Two II* (Wrecking Ball Press, 2003; illus. Van Howell). Many poems have been re-homed for this volume, in their more natural environments, which previous circumstances did not allow – sometimes re-grouped under fresh headings which more accurately reflect the provenance and flavour of the work. In addition to the 24 new poems in 'Jesus', a further 11 new poems are published here, sometimes under the heading of an earlier collection, as a late but hopefully improving addition to that previously published volume; all these new poems are marked with asterisks in the contents list.

Some of the *One Two II* twin lyrics were written for *One Two* (composer Gary Carpenter), developed by English National Opera Studio/Performing Arts Lab and showcased at Greenwich Theatre in 2001 and at ENO Studio's All-in-Opera Conference in 2000. Other lyrics are from *Shawna and Ron's Half Moon*, commissioned by ENO Studio (composers Ian McQueen et al) and performed at Hoxton Hall in 2000. Some 'Arrested Songs' were set to music by Rachel Leach and performed at Old Operating Theatre in 1998 as part of *Hard Cell*, an evening of prison writing. 'The Forgotten Muse', written for Christine Tobin, appeared on the cover of her CD *Deep Song* (Babel, 2000).

'Jesus' was commissioned by Poetry Proms, BBC Radio 3 (2002) and 'Umbrellas' by the Poetry Society. 'Professor' was a runner-up in the Arvon International Poetry Competition in 1998.

Acknowledgements are due to the editors of the following publications in which some of the uncollected poems first appeared: UK: *Poetry London*, *Poetry Review*, *Raw Edge*, *Ring of Words* (Sutton/Daily Telegraph), *Thumbscrew*; USA: *Kenyon Review*, *The Ledge*, *National Poetry Review*, *Terra Nova*; FRANCE: *Poésie Première*; SPAIN: *Sibila*.

The author is grateful to Arts Council Award 2003 and twice grateful to the Society of Authors for a grant in 1998 and 2004 Cholmondeley Award. Thanks also to the Royal Literary Fund: to Steve Cook and Hilary Spurling in particular, who were helpful above and beyond any call of duty, and to Jules Mann, U.A. Fanthorpe, Dr R. Bailey, Hugo Williams, David Morley, Gerard Woodward, William Meredith, Richard Harteis, Anne Rouse, John Rushby-Smith, Tom Paulin and Peter Porter.

To Dad, operatically,
and to Mom, for President

CONTENTS

JESUS

Your Room

Once a day,
go to your room,
alone of course

and with or without your supper
go
to your room now, and cry freely.
Cry loudly.
Embarrass the neighbours

into the unspoken thoughts.
The ancients understood
purpose in the sacrifice, which
– honest – isn't so terrible:
this going to your room, alone.

Our day and age,
especially this, our day and age,
needs its best town criers.

Don't finish too quickly.
Take extra care, running
the tongue across every
swollen inch of lip
to imprint the taste of one.

The wet, salty track
angling across your face
looks to lead you over
old, familiar dunes
and out to sea.

Later, it is a dry, salty track
which is how you know
for sure you are home.

Procrastinatin' Blues

You're not in love with lists, the kind
dead organised with a running jump on time.
No, that's not you. You're Eleventh Hour, right down to your toes.

The clock says eight – on time – so wait
'cause you'll be miserable until it's half-past eight
and you're Eleventh Hour, dear, still trackin' down your clothes.

You're feelin' pretty great!
Somewhere, in the musty recess of your mind there lurks a date
but that's weeks old, oh baby, that's how the Eleventh Hour goes.

A guy hangs loose, relaxed
while empires burn. You know that if we had a tardy tax
you'd be, for sure, Eleventh Hour – payin' big-time through the nose.

Don't you just hate
when pals don't show? Leave you standin' at the gate
Eleventh Hour Style? How dare they change the way the river flows!

Aw hell: better lay some bait
to get them out the door so *they're* the ones who'll have to wait
'cause don't you know, nothin' happens till the Eleventh Hour shows.

In case the clock is fast
and you surprise yourself on time, well, just keep walkin' past,
cross the street and walk Eleventh Hour Avenue, where no one knows.

Hey, there's cargo, and there's freight.
And which is which you'll never know – the hour's never late
until Eleventh Hour's gates swing open then swing back and start to close

– ain't it a crime –
with you the last behind the last in line
Eleventh Hour, not a soul behind. You can't deny the choice you chose.

Go on. Back-pedal at a frenzied rate,
but you'll still face an undone masterpiece. Consider fate
finally, now that it's the Eleventh Hour and a chill wind blows.

Piano Lesson

(to George)

It couldn't have been my Beethoven Bagatelle.
My jagged sprint from C to higher C,
with E a stepping stone, did not go well.
But something seemed to set those martins free.

Summer thread unspools the weathered barn
and then re-sews the rafters overhead;
although what seemed like joy must be alarm
maybe not at me, at my Bagatelle instead.

Heart of hearts, I willingly mis-heard.
My fingers dreaming fast but dragged along
had struck a bargain and I paid in birds
imprisoned by a crisis, not by song.

For shame – they soothed the eighth-notes' drunken lurch.
Birds, old barn: be my confessor's church.

Professor

In my study of female circumcision
Amongst the Sudanese tribes,
It has been interesting to note
That the procedure has no noticeable effect
On subsequent marriage and childbearing,
And that few side effects trouble the patient.
It's important to know how the women themselves
Champion the practice, or so I gather

When I am able to talk to them,
Which is not often,
Owing to the various tribes' particular codes of conduct
Which I am loathe to break.
However, I have asked them to describe the procedure –
The knife, the needles, the sutures, the aftercare –
Not because I take pleasure
In hearing about such things (needless to say)
But because there isn't the pain you'd expect.
They just go numb

As if the spirits have departed them
To race across the plains,
Trampling the dust of the plains
And disappearing over the edge of the world.

Innu

It's a habit now, –
seven hours of blank staring
until the TV map jerks west enough
for landfall, the very first: Goose Bay. Goose Bay.

I'm hooked on the sound.
Can't you just see it, startled congregants
of the coast, ignited into a glorious fire, a storm
of feather and the deafening gripes of warning or distress?

Goose Bay:
for the connoisseur of desolate land,
the connoisseur of the word, emptied of all but tundra,
icy waste. Now it's official: even their suicide rate soars romantically.

Who wishes to land
among the frozen garden dumps
to hear the parents say: *Take our children...Please.*
To meet these children grouped in the streets, laughing too loudly

breathing
from the garbage bags of gas
clutched to their chests like babies,
like a host of Iron Lungs keeping alive the already dead.

Jesus

*...As he sowed, some fell by the wayside...and some fell on stony
ground where...it had no depth of earth; But when the sun was up,
it was scorched; and because it had no root, it withered away.*
MARK, 4

Each time I went to Seville, I slept on the Street of Slaughter,
Street of the Scythe, with kind friends, less kind friends, who led me
down baroque naves, where I knelt at countless altars
I shouldn't have – Madrid, Salamanca – letting strangers wed me.

Who'd be a wandering Jew in a Jewless Jewish quarter?
Not Susona, whose skull I bore home in a paperweight
and who betrayed her people on her Christian lover's altar.
As reward, her Godly knight abandoned her to a Christian fate.

I believe that the convent life would suit not just nuns
because I gawp at Virgins' whites of eyes, at waxy Jesus babes,
– precious infants of formaldehyde, images of the son
of God, the only one – because this is how the childless are saved.

There were other summers, other trips, when I met head-on
a rare bearded vulture, the lammergeyer, one Pyrenean Spring.
I rounded a corner to that lamb killer's ten-foot wingspan
floating in on the hot, dry up draught early evening brings.

I'd waited for it already so long! with an ornithology teacher,
by the cliff escarpment nest, only the day before
but: *nada*. Now there it loomed. I too can drop live creatures
until they shatter to a heap of bones on the valley floor.

Santiago de Compestela they swore was never sunny.
A naughty child, I crept inside idolatry behind the altar,
inside the sanctuary – travesty of the Land of Milk and Honey –
seduced, like Susona, by incense, by St James, the notes of the Psalter,

by the polychrome and gilt smothering everything.
Talented at pilgrimage, I sank down, stroking paint
if not his face, fingering the hardened robes, and jewels and rings,
to get inside myself, outside myself, inside that stony Saint.

I managed summers away from churches, up mountains
or naked, baking on a shore, but mostly I drew breath
from the piazzas of orange trees and bougainvillaea, the tiled fountains
of the Barrio de Santa Cruz, the Maze of Death,

all my souvenirs of a kind: Leal's 'End of Glory',
with God tipping scales above Manara's corpse – worm-eaten,
   softened
(morbidity which made Murillo hold his nose – or some such story).
Repeatedly, I came upon myself in the Street of the Coffin.

Who'd be an aimless Jew in the Jewless Santa Cruz?
Might as well sit down. What passes over me yet leaves deep marks,
what passes through: communion in the bottles of cheap booze
being the time-honoured way to obliterate the dark.

I took my relics home, but left behind the child I'd never bear
in a smoky club, in Madrid, at 5 a.m. Of course, it rained.
I danced all night, let myself be led up marble stairs.
They seemed so beautiful, my countless deaths of Spain.

The Buddhas of Bamiyan

like the Venus de Milo,
are much more beautiful without their feet
but if your gaze soars upwards
how not too upward? How?

The Buddhas of Bamiyan
cannot compete with an authentic God,
should never bear the face of even the false God.
You, who are as arrogant as the usual man,
may love more deeply the pity of a headless,

footless Buddha of Bamiyan – even doubly so.
You, who can meditate only bodily,
don't deserve the pelvis of Buddha.
God is the greatest practitioner of art
and her favourite sculpture is a modest man.

Like the Venus de Milo
(if you are the man who dwells on her),
the twin Buddhas of Bamiyan
armless, can still embrace Afghanistan unbroken,
embrace those would would rather die than keep

each Buddha from divinity: its vanishing trick.
You who have a mind to, who can think as loftily
as the Buddhas of Bamiyan, can miss them but let them go.
Imagine all the fragments whole again,
and our signature on the empty sky.

Biology Cats
(for Karin)

If Bosch drew kites they'd look like this:
horrors, but for science class so coolly valid,

pinned at four paws, crucified,
nastily splayed across a palette
for our childish forensic exercise.

Taut-skinned, shiny, a study in tension,
they'd savagely tear with only a tiny intervention
from my lab-mate's exploring knife.

They'd trail behind me all my life
as I skipped along in the park,
each playful dip a windy prayer,

and later, they'd get tangled in my hair
or float above my head in the dark.

Gates as Gates, Not Symbols

It was a solid piece of craftsmanship.
It was a gate with no footholds – no notches,
no slats breaking up that jaunty facelessness
except way, way up at the top, much too high

where you'd arrive – where I did arrive one day –
where there was nothing to grab onto but the jolt of thin air

and the concrete wall the other side, shocking
solidity and roughness making mince of my chin,
and giving me the deepest sense of my bone.
It was raining. Of course. They opened the door,
mildly surprised and bewildered, so I became also
surprised and bewildered, whereas up until that point

I was just me inside myself, behind
that slash of blood, a tear-streaked mask, a pooling bruise.
They'd just been watching television, they told me.
The gate was unlocked, the gate was unlatched.

Couldn't I see? Nobody didn't want to let me in!
I saw something: the inflated hugeness of my sorrow.

I saw them sitting at their model family scene
with me crashing headfirst into their television,
framed unwillingly – I'd wrecked the crèche.
Not for the first time, and not for the last.
My plan was to live the rest of my hopefully long, deliriously
happy life, minus each damn one of them

but now here they are again, opening the door
on me, just standing there with their look of faint surprise.

The Literal and the Metaphor

Lover
or not of poetry,
you rehearse an impressive show as a lover
of women

and you're a natural with your line
in line
breaks.

Practices

We all have our peculiar rituals.
I'll be burning every unseen letter
until the neighbours phone the firemen.

There isn't any smell of meat or food,
no sign of skewers of the literal kind.
So when they come, how will I explain myself?

A petty, coward's version of Joan of Arc
where I don't burn, but only all the words
I'd rather see as cinders and as ash?

Or the pagan in me lusting, burning Guys,
celebrating when at last his head explodes
with fireworks – this is one I like!?

Better, candles floating in a bath,
enough of them to make a church of loss
and I'm just supplicant to scent and water.

Better, torch processions on the shore
signaling to someone how the living burns
even though, apparently, anything I burn

will never reach the far-off you: you,
the one I'm burning all these pages for.
When you come, how will I explain myself?

Handed Sunflowers

A field of them, each bloom
fat and powerful and devouring all space.
I could lean my whole weight
on a single trunk-like stem,
one cheek against one plush brown centre
– dense meat not unlike an open palm.

Fields and fields of them, hosts,
enough to make a cradle for us all,
enough to let us walk across
the way you'd walk on water, when it's dark.
They're fringed with yolk-coloured petals
you'd no more call petals
(something fragile, ephemeral)
than I'd call the fingers petals, your fingers petals.

We know what always happens later, don't we:
the end-of-summer collections of Southern France,
crowds waiting some thirty years in vain
for the bands of Woodstock, psychedelica faded.
And very, very tired by now, slouched
and empty-handed under a burning sun.

No fields, just three he bought me,
huge and weighty as the most magnificent lie.
Each kitchen pass, the scouts push out
– vast armies bent on their invasion.
It seems that the table can hardly hold that mass
but really it is me most likely to buckle and break.

A Pint

After me, the girls got smaller:
first an inch shorter
and then an inch less wide,
so slow, you'd hardly know the difference.

It was a good idea to wrap them
in your arms, deep as possible
so nothing flopped out in the bitter cold.
Not a foot. Not an elbow.

Nothing need ever be missing,
or nothing that anyone would notice.

The pace picked up, way past ridiculous,
his spanning of waists with special corsetry
to produce the tiniest of girls
all with the right, approximate, parts.

It was wrong of me – and far-fetched –
to think he could have made them small himself
with his own two hands!

Where did he find all these pint-sized girls?!
And when they'd achieved Petite
– At last! The Delightfully Miniature! –
their green eyes flashed like fireflies in a jar.

Drink-less, they'd squirm at parties,
their pretty squeaks from some side-pocket
gone past human hearing.

He'd flourish them at brief airings
as a treat – they'd be admired by assembled company.

Ah, they were Perfection itself, tickling
his palm, fluttering so delicately,
except there were no wings of course.

The Having of the Cake

Women in their 30s aren't meant to mourn for dogs or cats.
Scorned for their deflection of ancestral destiny
and less than free, they stand there while old friends reduce them
        to old bats
far in advance of any such disturbed reality.

He burdens her with images of someone gross and elderly
stuffed into short, tight skirts, accentuating all the fat,
with images of missing woman's destiny – he burdened me,
his feet up on a desk, and made his cruelty resemble tact.

The girls with babies clutch them close, and blessedly.
The boys arrange their separate lives, convenient flats
both north and south (an urban nest, a nest in the country)
and wait for 45, and newer girls with wombs entirely intact.

Please don't assume in reading this you know the facts:
that of a woman scorned, or some such tritely mournful history.
Can I explain and still refrain from tiresome, polemical tract,
myself, who looks beyond that man, or before this man unhappily?

I can't stand to love a loss of self, nor stand not loving best, devotedly,
him, with the sort of passion reason can't refract;
or him, with the sort of reason lack of passion throws at me
so bitterly, like corpses strewn across the forward path.

For the final dressing up, before I take my perfect leave,
I try on all the gloves and dresses, all the habits, all the hats
with a female's love of covering possibilities.
And I would try a thousand lives and loves as well, just like that.

Did I say female? Female to despair of all you lack?
To want forgiveness for living so imperfectly?
Did I say female, to want the knick as well as knack
of being female and astray, yet always welcomed back?

The Lost Mushrooms of Bologna

Down one slightly tattered pocket of Via Zamboni
(or some such street, since I pluck from Italian air
one square from a patchwork of titles),
maybe even at the pinkie finger's topmost crook
or into even smaller passages
lightly basted with graffiti,
past colonnade after colonnade,
past jumbled walls,
past stacked terracotta
of lemon and stained creamy rose:
dusty toys split by fault-lines
too like the clumsy scrawl of a broken heart
you wouldn't catch me dead inscribing for anyone, anywhere
– what am I saying? –

and, well, down any old street refined
by the strong desire for romantic fare,
through an alley as small as the place in the mind
reserved for such enormous lives residing there,

there nestles that bag of Porcini
– Boletus, as I say – never missed until we're hours older,
when another twenty planes have traced the route behind us,
their trails long evaporated into blue ice
much like the lurid pastel cocktail I should have ordered.

A woman in mink strides past, part of no adventure,
and then an army of furred ladies
I feel I should be loudly applauding
possibly to the accompaniment of brass instruments.
Like a poster-art de Chirico, they swerve through columns,
becoming the shadows of columns and then themselves.

There goes one now, sadly de-minked, to her kitchen,
alone, organised for only her sake
since the man affording minks has gone.
She roams the stainless steel of her kitchen,
spans a vast sink with manicured hands.

She spotted the mushrooms, but even in an empty hour
would never, never stoop to take them,
no matter how lost those mushrooms of Bologna.

Nor can we see the not-very-attractive ambling dog
attached to a middle-aged man (for example),
either of whom may or may not aim a desultory sniff
in the mushrooms' direction – an easy mistake
considering the meaty texture, the crowded presentation.
But they've missed them! A crying shame!

Having squeezed through a tiny door in the students' quarter,
where he is happily overstaying his educational welcome,
the ageing student unhooks the leash, removes his shoes.
The apartment is narrow, lived in,
with a tang of wet dog and dirty linen.
Is this sad? A dog greatly loved? No television?

The dinner peppers are wilted
with crinkled papery skin, like the skin
of his mother's arm, his mother's upper arm.
He reads the same books again and again,
musing on the Baroque when it's too Baroque,
on the cartoonish quality of early religious art.
He's in love with the almond-eyed Madonnas
which people his city. He theorises
how they inhabit Modigliani, perhaps even more
than they inhabit his own sighs.

Is this even sadder? I must stay longer.
But he doesn't even exist!
He missed the mushrooms and the peppers miss
the mushrooms too. This is no ordinary hunger.

There's one housewife who picks them up,
takes them to her bosom (as it's said)
examines from all angles the bag
and what it appears to be. Intact.
Then she tells her husband, a heavy man with a red face
who returns them to their place
(in this fiction, such things are even probable).

He might have offered her a husbandly whack
on the back of her head, for picking up rubbish like that,
or maybe he just sank in a chair with a paper,
not nasty, but agonisingly inert,
fixed with a gloom both searing and banal.
It goes without saying she cooks without mushrooms.
Unusually, neither is there any dessert.

So anything else to exhibit? Anything else to feel?
Anything else made by distance equally real?
Down the old cobbled seam which holds together
the middle of the road, I pick my delicate way in heels
as if it's a shingle beach, where a wrong move could hurt
and deliver me up to the hands of strangers.

Cautious, or staring at an inconsequential window
as apt as not to reveal a florid ceiling tracery,
I've ground to a halt
when the hornet of a motorbike
buzzes our absent forms sideways, back to England

from where I'd like to address
my lost mushrooms of Bologna, as one does
or, rather, the way one doesn't, not nearly enough of the time
since most losses are unaccountable, unnoticed.
How many years would it take to unwind
all the alternatives? To write them
with a flourish, an attention to detail never found in life?

There's time for only the one – the one
which takes us back to England
with one portion of recall for those forgotten,
the one concerning a few lost mushrooms,
dried, cramped in plastic
with no further growing hopes
even in their habitual dark,
nor the hope of dignity in a broth's more public performance.
They hold our place like a bookmark.

Unless they're marked out for a modest resurrection,
unless the bag gets eagerly torn away,
its contents revived and tossed

into its proper end, a proper risotto chemistry,
in the way that mistakes and loss
turn out to be the truest destiny of all.
Let's hope so, either way, and since

I'd like to think it good to mourn
what there is to mourn,
– that is: most of what came before –
and maybe love one thing we happen across.

Bookmark

(for Ken & Judi)

I heard about the apple blossom
on the air-waves – a rare,
a singular long spell
of it, they said – an afterlife –
down to last year's rain.

I never think of that,
how the weather's work
long past pays dividends
and how the ghostly silhouettes
renew the vows. I wasn't first

to note how long the shoulders
wore the crumbling lace, but once
I had, I had to hold the page
for all late-risers, dreamers
moving on, and missing it.

RSPCA

Let me tell you how some things happen:
One day, you've turned into the household cat
pretty bad at bagging birds
but sidling up to a creature hurt enough
to be caught in your small, pincer jaws.
You head indoors, make an aviary of the sitting room

at which point, and where, you become yourself,
mad matador brandishing towels
but still the bird shrugs off the dark,
his wings a hurricane of flutter and flap
and oh god, he's hurled himself against the window pane
with a thud, until it's streaked with shit.
That sound! So hard to bear while you brace yourself

as you've been told, to grip him tight through cloth,
performing finally the trick of the towel
in a room dimmed by shut curtains, unfinished light.
You thought you'd had the very worst, the very best
as hunter, witness and saviour
but lastly, it's your task to be that bird
huddled in a corner, over and over, in all corners
of every room – aviary, study, play-pen, prison –

or launching yourself towards a mirage of open air
in a world where windows do not exist.

Off the Back of a Lorry

Whatever he owns,
    whatever he has ever owned
fans out either side of him
    in a peacock's tail, or lengthens behind
in the breadcrumb trail
through darkening woods
to the gingerbread house.

Trousers flap away from motor-bikes.
Umbrellas nestle
    beneath bars,
and lighters wriggle down behind the cushions of a lover's couch.
Pens leap two families
or more
to home in a shopkeeper's pocket
...Jackets,
    underwear,
        numbers
for business, affairs,
land up in wrong streets, on skewed chairs.
His daughter's gift
    slips
        through a gap in the door.

It must be wrong
    to hoard a traveller's signs
but who believes
    in unbothered
        loss?
Even ghosts have reputations,
however hollow.

He nurtures something vast
    and unnerving,
a talent for the quickened versions of inheritance, directed
by circumstance
and never
    to the children,
        never to the deserving.

A lyrical image surfaces:
    the wake
of a trawler
    gone
        from harbour this moment
with every desire
for its ports of call as open as the sea which swallows it up.

Let's not follow that word:
    Wake.
        Lose it
before it over-stretches enticement.
Lose it.
    Before
        it loses itself.

Summer Salad

In it were slices of malachite
like cucumber, chunks of fresh jade-avocado,
lapis drops too wet to clasp on my ears
and way down below, buried rubies for radishes.

At first, I was reluctant to eat so wastefully,
toyed with the wooden implements
while everyone else tucked in, and gorged,
unbothered by eating heaps of jewels.

To stall, I turned to a side dish,
lifted a giant potato from out of its bowl.
For admiration. But it was tough, inedible.
I satirised Atlas, and no one laughed.

I guess it was better than letting them go,
eating that glorious rainbow of stones.
So here I am, adding shavings of orange agate like carrot,
crisp quartz, carnelian, every precious thing I own.

Gallery

(for Anne)

When I become like these people
once hung on my walls with innocent pleasure
and an eye for eccentricity as a palliative,

when I become the Pre-Raphaelite lady
kneeling to unwrap a wooden cat on wheels
while his lighter shadow, alive
and licking his paws, waits on the sill,

when I become the jaded lank-haired lush
propping up the bar – her fag
like a drooping cock still braving it,
like a missile about to misfire –

become the pastel face of a hungry child,
a Victorian child locked out of home and dream,
bound by trellis and powdery flowers –

or become the one trying too hard as a clown –
white-ruffed, embracing a mandolin
which will always be silent as snow...
when I become like them, like that

the way you begin to look like your dog
and also begin to look like your house, or it like you,

when I become like them, like that,
well, then, I do. And that's all there is to it.

The Letters I Never Sent

The miniature islands littering the sea,
uninhabited, but each with its community
of closed oysters, the fan-like debris
of the tides, elegant as parlour embroidery.

Some tornadoes never reach the ground,
whipping up an air which doesn't count.
Swept up in that unnoticed passion:
a telephone, a lousy noun, a weeping sound.

Nothing can compare, seem better than
the wear and tear of constant measuring.
Repeatedly, I tune the cello strings
but someone else will bring the weather in.

The folly of an ancient, brittle atlas.
Some die to map an error – although France
was once an unknown concept, not a task.
What commander is without her past?

Disappointing Tomatoes

Deceptively red, inviting,
like those ones to which all others must be compared,
those others purchased in a lost, warm place,
yet they've not delivered on promise.

Familiar?
And speaking of.

Spilling over the edge of the season,
not legendary yet,
should they not still impart great things

of their late age?

They, not yet missed, not yet numbered
among the fallen,
not yet numbered among the dead.

They should.
They do. Remember?

Not deceptive.
Sweet.
Among the living
among us.

Umbrellas Along a Canal

Coloured parasols
charred by an evening drizzle.

Black mushrooms, nightmare-grown.

Voting booths
for elections by thunder.

Full stops

when the water is a sentence
without punctuation

and only a single thing to say.

It's always the train
turns me into the stuttering one,

and strewn behind me,
all those unopened gifts.

This Book

Before it's stung by wasps
or devoured by lions,
for the shortest of times

I carry it around with me
from one room to the next,
not every day, but some days

I could only begin to describe
without belabouring the new-born
or stretching the point of emptiness.

No one can know I do this,
squeezing it to death, holding it
like a fan of playing cards

hugged close to the chest,
like it's more me than me, or a lover,
its cover glossy and so cold.

MASQUES: MUSES & SONGS

Can Clio do more than amuse?

Say, for what were hop-yards meant,
Or why was Burton built on Trent?
Oh many a peer of England brews
Livelier liquor than the Muse.
And malt does more than Milton can
To justify God's ways to man.

A.E. HOUSMAN

Interlude

Thalia and Melpomene meet at The Queen's Head
by pure chance. Both dressed in second-hand suits,
they light each other's fat cigars. Then after,

they stagger home, strip off, pose on the bed
in a pantomime of woman/man pursuits.
Unable to make it, they dissolve in tears and laughter.

The Necessary Voyeur

There he is, the third party, the watcher,
the spare prick at the wedding,

leaning over the lit glass-case,
its exquisite illumination.

Urania had some errands to run
so the husband's minding the shop.

And does he mind? A glimpse of heaven,
flesh on the verdigris bedspread,

the lapis criss-cross rail of veins
on the lovers' hands, clutching

at the binary system he longs to break
with a stroke of his staff over the globe.

Are you Sirius? he makes her joke
while her lover's turning her over.

By the time the wife returns
he's carried away with Orion's belt,

her begging, begging him not to leave.
She needs him to do what she does.

Irish Lover

Erato's twin brother, dead at birth,
full-grown, with a hurley in his fist
left a ghost to field women's passion.

She weighs those hide-bound cork balls
in a matchless game which swells him proud.

Pinning row on row of butterflies,
he who deftly miscued towards the cushion
and struck off-centre to ignite her fire

is lying on his back, of two minds
about her loving his gentle power to withdraw.

After Verlaine

My lovers are not literary types.
They are labourers on building-sites.
They build houses and dig drains.
They do not sip champagne.

I want their strong arms to pin me to the bed.
I want them to enjoy me without romance,
simply, the way they take their beer and bread
I want to make them hard and make them dance.

They do not own a tie or fancy shirts, or a single suit.
Their bodies have an earthy scent
or reek of cheap cologne like Brut.
Their hands are rough and thick, and elegant.

They're not so hot at grammar, except in bed
where suddenly every word they say is correctly said.
They may not wash sometimes but breathe me in
as if my skin were made of oxygen.

They trail a tang of sweat and stale tobacco everywhere.
Unfinished at the edges, they don't wear underwear.
All they do is belch and fuck and hawk and fart.
They can't tell the difference between their prick and their heart.

Euterpe Descending

Euterpe: muse of Dionysiac music, inventress
of the double flute, patroness of joy and pleasure.

When her usual magic had failed,
she took to bed and slept. For a change.
She, once in charge of flutes and pleasure,
could hardly smile or open her arms
or mouth the words expected of lovers.

There she lay, rigid and nailed
to her back, not by passion's exchange,
not by anything she could measure.
Her thoughts set off Olympian alarms.
She was longing, burning for another.

She remembered a lake she'd sailed,
a ride as divinely disarranged
as the sky, the water, the weather.
Let memory do her no harm.
Let passion help her recover.

Let the sailor come back and love her.

An Epic in Me

So that the telling may not be diverse from the fact
DANTE

Sweating, his body becomes hot wax
moulding me. I want my impression to last.

The weight of him is a team of horses
lumbering over a wooden bridge,

shoving, shoving on the advance guard.
Not quite bravery, but eloquent brawn.

He runs whole pitches through the night.
A hundred "tries", he's no closer to goal.

Making his mark deep inside of me,
he stitches the laces of a cross, a dash —

he who loathes the intellectual.
With him I felt sublimely wordless. Until this.

Muse of Blues

I was usin' a carving knife
down any number of men.
Maybe it was someone I knew
way, way back when.

I was feelin' kinda blue.

I was in a helluva rush,
sweepin' whole armies away
with a Straight and Royal Flush..
I was ace with rocks, ace with lead,
cuttin' the giants to shreds

Gimme a break, okay?
I was feelin' kinda blue.

Wouldn't you?

All that's for becomin' the boss.
All that, to be havin' a ball
wond'rin' what was it for.
To be laid on my nice pine floor,
flattened to the shape of a cross.
To cry for 'em all.

The Male Polyhymnia Turns to Crime

Though his voice is enthralling, deep
as water pooled in a gorge,
with a timbre, warm
as bees, thrumming to the heat,

it simply isn't good enough.
He's jealous of his noble brother Calliope.

Why should he be doomed to harmony
sotto voce, singing a supporting role,
penning sweet daffodil riffs for spinsters,
tired psalms, mumbled out of tune, low church?

He boils at a vision: the aproned helpmeet
serving condiments for the great chef.

A signature from Euterpe
on a calling card's mosaic of notes
earns a date with Clio.

A weekend's booked in Paris where
he plans to show her what he's made of, once
and for all, show her that he's not to be taken
lightly, or in vain.

Remembering Before Forgetting

You're the controlling type
and that's bad for love.

You insist on a script, even in bed,
and that's bad for love.

You delegate all the boring tasks
by default – bad for love.

You're always inside your head
and that's bad for love.

You're cheap with presents – you never ask
and that's bad for love.

You're grim by day and grim by night
and that's bad for love,

very bad for love.
That's bad, that's love.

The Muse of Spleen

May your lovers bite you hard and deep,
tattoo you with musical staves.
May they play cold whore to your knave
and then like schoolgirls sleep.

May they laugh at your jokes, burn the toast,
accidentally swallow the host.

May your potent songs astound
with their seduction leitmotif.
May the silken scarves be beautifully bound
around your tactical brief.

May the girls all play their girlish role,
rule shyly, then boldly relinquish control.

May they take in their tiny hands
your swelling reputation.
May I use my tiny hands
in a different celebration

accompanied by this sexual psalm.
May the truth collect like rain in our palms.

The Hypochondriacal Muse

All that I am hangs by a thread tonight
ANNA AKHMATOVA

Clio's battery of tests yielded nothing
but a fin de siècle pain in the side.

All he can think of is hospital error.
He scratches his arm, then freezes in terror

at whatever he cannot make sense of:
scored tongue, the blood's ebbing tide,

sclerosis, cirrhosis – a boomerang synapse
and he's dead on target for total collapse,

hounded by symptoms he cannot control.
No wonder he cannot make love!

There *is* an unusual heat, lead in the pipes,
the body politic poisoned by clype.

Quick! To bed, for a generation
of so much diviner operations!

Euterpe longs to marry flesh with the soul,
while passion to him is a moment's reprisal,

a footnote, screened in the heart's tiny chancel.
Will needles in the groin make him whole?

Terpsichore Twice

At Sousa's Music School on Baltic Street
they jabbed his fingers wrapped around a flute.
They made him kneel and fumble at the nest
of drums, or, seated, stumble over the piano keys
like upended coffins littering the open seas
where all the music of the world is put to rest.
When he broke a bone on the playground chute
they sacked him from the kindergarten fleet.

For what was he if he couldn't even dance?
A failure, no-hoper. He wouldn't stand a chance
but for these bodies made like instruments
carved from passion rather than good sense,
and since he could embrace this cello's girth
he played well, to pin me to the earth.

Possible Muses

Out back, out there

imprisoned by generous neighbours,
the only apron of earth I own
reveals a summer pattern

of blind fuchsia and blind snails.
I never iron, and what greenery lives
lives despite this stunning hand.

But let me tell you about the uninvited guests
for I set their place at table without fail.

Such a good custom for hosts
whose three graves are tucked in a corner
like border stitching:

one for me, one for my better self
and one for my lover, for you
who do not yet know who you are.

Unspeakable Muse

Mostly, it's music-hall, or trivia like that,
tin-pot, mouth-comb, the spoon and pail.

I've flecked his beard with soup,
or placed a piece of spinach in his teeth,
Off-days, you'll find me lazily
unzipping a fly or two.
There are appointments
to tuck prim matrons' skirts
inside their underwear.

You used to like it. You always did. Until

one day I refused one whitish lie,
and then I called us on your words
or worse: the silences.

I reel in an entire underwater habitat.
Truth burns a hole in the bed,
and anger is the first and now the only lover.

When I won't let go, you pull that knife
made to fit against my throat.
You may ask why I persist with these dares.
Even now, you wouldn't take my life!

Mneme Recovers the Wrong Memory

first by skirting warm shores a whole summer,
giving rivers, the Pont du Gard, a miss – each whiff of thyme
and lavender breath disdained...you small and hiding

in what shade was thrown from cracked and brittle eaves,
beneath the fig tree I was stripping of leaves
for my namesake, persistent, along for the ride.

You were wet, even in the dry Garrigue.
Four times I refused to be your bride.
Always, you'd rather mope at home, cold, in need,

even to dream of these very same foothills
in their deepening absence, away from it all,
the way these foothills dream of the mountains

which are both their father and son
and the Alps dream of the war these foothills won.
You should have rejoiced at our smoking car

stalled nowhere near medieval squares
in that nowhere no-how frontier town:
you who could corner the dark at the highest noon

with affordable misery, your litany of colds,
and your practised talent at being old.
We were a weekend away from back in control,

a lengthening weekend away from spare parts,
way, way off the map, with our angry hearts.
Leave it to you to kill the joy among the ruins!

I'm tracking it down, past the faded tourist stars,
the wartime plaques...tracking it down. Not feeling well?
Let's meet again, shrunk down in their worn armchairs,

the elderly Resistance, now hard-of-hearing
and ghosts at their own last chance hotel.
Mute, and chewing and peering

at a massive dusty TV screen from a distance,
they hardly move to motion us down the echoing halls
towards iron bedsteads facing blank walls,

the naked bulbs, the peeling paint no one will mend.
The miracle of drink will always make us friends
with the dying, friends with the sad and the old.

In which case, was this not the time of your life?!
Despair with your almost, almost ex-wife
who was leading you right to the living end?

I craned my head from the back of our leaving car:
Goodbye wasteland, beautiful hell. Save my fading place.
I was lifted by a floating holiness in the desert. From far,

far away, in the future, I push into your face
the lovely nurse wiping your nose with a kiss:
she in love with those who love all lovers of deep night.

Not me! But speaking of the future, by then, slowly,
slowly, as if underwater, it will swing into bliss
too late – it will sing. Summer. The enduring myth.

Mneme Re-writes History

I'm so damn tired of love for the dead,
of the lies of the living about their dead.

Minus the bodily subject of their praise,
they dig up corpses of buried words,
powder the vowels, adjust the consonant limbs
and prop them up on silk pillows.

They take into their mouths cold lips
with passion, finally, for their own grief.

Grave Melete

A bracing frightener, both live and dead,
I'd wrap waxy fingers around the feeble throat

of the funeral singer and the eulogy writer
daring to twist memory into their touching notes

sung for the false, sung for the barely living.
They're moved by belief in the dead forgiving:

those who cannot ever again say: *no*.
Ever again. And then I'd have to let go.

Terpsichore in Training

For guests I acted out my family part,
tripped lightly, mindful of her glass grisaille
lined up on the mantelpiece, a veritable city.
It reeked of formula: if I failed, she failed,
and this gave me the will to please if not the heart.
So I turned the empty gestures into something pretty,
risked sentiment with the deepest, darkest curtsy,
twisted into shape by her cash blackmail.

What a vastly overcomplicated debt!
I spot her zimmer, smile and mean it more
now the jewels are clouded, the bed is wet.
I surprise myself, an actress to the core.
We sip from the cracked bone-china tea-set.
The nurse hands me my shawl, shows me the door.

Urania's Royal Mission

(On confusing the death of Princess Diana with the occasion of the first photos from the surface of Mars)

For this muse:
a slow crawl
along red soil
towards an ordinary rock.

After a years-long
voyage:
astral fame.
A stopped clock.

The Forgotten Muse

(for Christine)

Who said they'd take the song over the singer?
Those choosing love instead of choosing the lover?
More than once, I burned a sheet of my words,
to cast a spell. Nothing was ever recovered.

from

ONE TWO II:
TWINS & SONGS

When one becomes two, what will you do?
– attributed to Jesus, Gospel of St Thomas

HELEN'S SISTER

Twins

There are two versions of all you desire,
both nearly the same.

A butterfly
and a butterfly in rain.

The Rorschach test.

Desire breeds that butterfly with its wing
minus the piece which is everything,

a butterfly veiled by rain.

Helen's Sister

Once they know I'm beauty's twin
at the party door, I'm in,

if only so they can compare
roses to hips hardened by winter air.

Nine months perfectly in tune
with the sharer of our mother's womb –

you'd think that beauty's shadow would earn
one brief victorious public turn.

In Sparta, I'd be second-rate,
without a date,

and if in my part of Athens
nothing much happens

(even the migrating birds
like euphemistic words

or an air-blown lover's kiss
– false and paltry – give this part of town a miss)

still, I'm a big fish in a tiny pond,
twin to a natural blonde

but at least a reference for men's desire,
the heat of the missing fire.

While our strong and handsome brothers
wrestle with each other

on top of Ulysses' mast
(male ego, vanity and brass!)

it's Helen's Fire completes the sum,
for she's the portent of the worst to come.

She's the corposant which starts
the charge between all lovers' parts.

If beauty's an affliction,
then men and women love addiction.

Here, the evening creeps
across the place where my lovers sleep

then rise to leave me instead
once daylight steals the Helen that I'd had them bed.

When it comes to beauty, the world knows best
and the Trojan war's the test.

Any woman would slay a thousand soldiers
not to get older.

Twins Two

A

There are two versions of all you desire,
both nearly the same:
the heat just before the break into fire,

a butterfly in rain.
The Rorschach Test.

B

The Rorschach test:

One wing is gold and blue and best
and the other wing is gold and blue and best.

Desire breeds a butterfly veiled in rain,
two versions of all you desire.

The Old One Two

I send him on a mission
to do the things I wouldn't do
with loaded ammunition.

He can tell the lie
and act disgracefully
while I stand calmly by.

Starting from birth
I had two minutes upper hand
which multiplied my worth.

Strange as it may seem,
to him and me both equally
I was the stronger of the team

– older, smarter and more ethical.
I could call him on all wrongs
(mainly hypothetical).

For he was born to fail
to save the pain and trouble
from the more successful male.

While he could have a lover
bodily, her heart and soul
fell always to the other.

When I would steal the sweets,
he'd take the rap while
sweetly I'd retreat.

His gestures mirror mine,
so I can know the pleasure
not the punishment from crime.

I've heard that most of us
leave in our mother's womb
a duplicate, a ghost

perhaps just two months old
or less – a minute's life
perpetually on hold,

which accounts for our despair.
The search for missing twins
goes on everywhere.

Envy my twin's fate,
a brother to success and love,
always too early, always too late.

The Rorschach Test

There are two versions of all you desire,
two versions of all you desire,

both nearly the same:
the spark a second before the break into fire,
a book with facing pages nearly the same

– the page of pleasure facing the page of pain –
the binary system of zero and one,
what you did and what you might have done,

the butterfly with or without the rain.
The Rorschach test.

One wing was gold and blue and best
and the other wing was gold and blue and best
but somehow different from the rest.

Desire's template is a butterfly with its heart
minus a piece right from the start...

Here is the test:
when the missing piece is discovered
then fitted, the other wing loses a corner,

like lovers, like mourners,
like zero without the one,
two stars and what you might have done.

Then there are three versions of all you desire,
three versions of all you desire,

all you desire.

Doppelgänger

They say that on the day when he appears,
the day you're face to face with your own double,
subtract your remaining days and years.

From the very start, dear brother, I was troubled.
Nine months before drawing a single breath
I was living with my own death.

Hand in Glove

(Rastafarians don't say 'we' but 'I And')

Make me the hand
and you the glove.

The shifting of sands.
The mechanics of love.

It might be a curse
underneath the blessing.
The pleasure, the undressing.

The ecstatic, misty view
always gets cold,
with the 'I' in the 'you'.

The hand may learn to hate its glove
for keeping it warm.

The illusion of calm
in the unit of two.

Be both the hand and the glove,
hand in glove.
The mechanic of love.

The Twin's Seduction Line

Pretend I'm her, pretend she's me.
I'm nearly her: the other shoe.
That's what people always do.

Pretend that what's in front of you
is someone else altogether.
Make flesh and blood the 'if' and 'whether'.

Toss out the old – rent something better.
Gods prefer their ones in twos.
Then explain: it was all confused.

Pretend I'm her, pretend she's me.
I'm nearly her: the other shoe.
That's what people always do.

ARRESTED

Narcissus Reflects
(to Gary)

One nymph's as good as another.
Perhaps I'm being unfair.
I've been through so many Goddesses.
I've searched everywhere.
I've searched high, I've searched low.
Can I find them? No!
Just fatal flaws and oddnesses.

Eurydice moped in the dark.
You know the type, in love with despair,
a black cloud blocking her charms.
Thetis had lovely long wavy hair.
Alas, that was under her arms.

Amphritite lived in the sea
and a nymph who ruins her skin is a fool.
Clytie was, well, exceptionally tall.
Galatea was hot but uncool.

My last amour was Syrinx
who'd passed through the hands of Pan
before he turned her into a pipe.
You blow as hard as you can.

One nymph's as good as another.
Perhaps I'm being unfair.
I've tried loving so many Goddesses,
it hasn't got me anywhere.
Have I found love? No such luck.
Will I find love? *Will I – fuck.*

The Longest Sentence

There's a charge of failing to indicate left
and added to that, resisting arrest.
There's just a small matter of dangerous driving,
missing a court date, then finally arriving
tanked up from your liquid-lunch session.
Unlikely, to drop the cocaine possession,
in fact, we'll extend this sentencing session.

There are charges of running off at the mouth
and gesturing crudely the direction of south,
missing the punch-line of too many jokes,
boring to tears your wife and her folk.
That time through customs you should have declared
those purple nylon underwear...

Because the sad truth is you're deeply unstylish,
not to mention illiterate, Irish.
That time you believed every siren for you
was just paranoia   and unluckily true.
From birth you've resisted, resisted arrest.
You might as well get your life off your chest.

Your sworn full confession
will endeth this lesson.

A Short Sentence

No one is innocent
excepting the judge.
It's a tough life, isn't it?
And worse, with a grudge.

So use your time well.
Write in your journal
– if you can spell.
And don't take it personal.

Complaining Litany

Oh, Guv, of Thy Heavenly Bounties deprive me not...

I told you I'm clean.
The jewellery was hot
but the guy who got shot
was nothing but rot.

It wasn't my plot
and I swear it was not
my killing machine.

Time's past and I'm clean,
not nearly as mean
as some guys I've seen...

O Guv, deliver me from the eternal tormentors...

Grub out to tender,
another shit winter,
the shits at the Centre,

discussions of gender,
do-gooder mentors,
the time which I lent her...

Time less like a stinter
and more like a sprinter.
The letters I send her

returned to the sender.
Dear John and Dear John...
Oh, what are you on?!

Oh, what are you on?!

Returned to the sender.
Tonight's for a bender.
I ain't no offender.

O Guv, sprinkle into my heart the dew of Thy grace...

Not the pig-ugly face
of my cell-mate, that waste
who takes up my space.

Not another paper-chase
when it comes to my case.

Not another paper-chase
when it comes to my case.

The dew of thy grace?
Just a little more space!

Just a little more space!

Who really cares
for all of us thugs
with bad dispositions?

The Sun really cares!

It's my suspicion
the Telegraph wears
its snotty derision
disguised as a 'vision'.

So the Governor said
that too much bread
would go to our heads.

It would go to our heads!

No television
was the next wise decision
made by the mugs
sitting upstairs.

They block information,
hint at release
then the very next week
do a sentence increase.

Back on the drugs
after remission:
adjudication.

Adjudication!

Those wise older lags
they give me the rag
and offer me fags,
some good porno mags

A believable blag
to earn me Home Leave,
Chapel Orderly Job
One Day Release

Bloody peace!

Some phone-cards to rob.
Parole not referred...
I'll add to the list
of things that I miss

and things that I wish:
an easier bird.
No rollcall at all,

having the balls
to stand up to staff,
holding onto my laugh.

Having my sentence reduced.
Birds who are loose
and early release.
Bloody peace.

Bloody peace!

O Guv, give me humility, chastity and obedience...

(You can skip on the chastity
part of the equation...)
Just set me free.

Set me free!

O Guv, deliver me from every temptation...

(Except Female Officer Dray...

Female Officer Dray!
blows 'em away...)

But who am I fooling
with this panting and drooling.
Here I am, tied and tagged!
Locked up and gagged.

That's it, in the bag.

O Guv, deliver me to just a few small temptations,
a pound of pleasure, an ounce of elation.

O Guv of thy heavenly bounties, we're more of the same,
no better, no worse than anyone else you could name.

The Oxford University Press, in Hospital

As befits an afflicted poet
nearing an operative time,
I lay in the ward Robert Bridges
who was doctor of men and of rhyme.

Nearby hung poetic displays
of the Laureate's history at Bart's.
(My surgeon was moved to comparisons
– *two* poets of extraordinary parts.)

With hours and days trudging past,
my fantasies proved my best fun:
catalogues of errors and brain damage,
death, and needles in the bum.

With hours to kill, I examined
the Victorian Bridges's bearded face,
the old photos of Great Ormond Street
and his London Caledonian base.

But most, what caught my attention
was the panel furthest to the right:
acknowledgments to venerable bodies
who'd brought this history to light.

First: here's the borough of Islington
who donated biographical news.
There are various hospitals thanked
for their 19th century views.

Lying there, wincing from sutures,
my body collapsed, a right mess,
one name in particular stood out:
Oxford University Press.

I'd run through the worst countless times,
practised well how I would expire
to make them feel good and sorry
for having me callously fired.

I'd entertained all the options
which keep hypochondriacs amused,
then realised it's worst scenarios
which keep coffin-chasers enthused.

Are you sick, feeling down, Literati?
Are you feeling kind of dead, or depressed?
Well then you're assured of a publishing run
with Oxford University Press.

Haven't you heard it's the fashion
to decline the hale and the hearty,
snub the living and only invite
the dead to the scholarly party.

Celebrate the germs and the scalpels
for they will be making your name.
The sicker you feel the more brightly
will shine that celestial fame.

Hurrah for dead, dying poets,
sick of consumption or gassed!
Murdered and cold in their grave,
at least they've an interesting past.

So here's a frank, open address
made from a hospital bed;
I'd rather be living unpublished
than be published by you and be dead.

Midtown Muzak

(with no apologies to Louis MacNeice and his 'Bagpipe Music')

It's no go, up Fortieth Street,
it's no go, say the East Side cops.
Before the horse and the baton bars,
that's where the people stop.

It's no go, you West Side lot,
the Uptown and the Downtown crew.
Go home to your e-mail husbandry
or we'll ride our horses straight over you.

It's no go, on the Battery ferries,
for a buck or two or not much more
tour the lady who loves us the most,
though a little bit less if you're hungry and poor.

It's no go, Grand Central Station,
it's no go – next train's the Pity,
a cancelled service and no way out
or into the heart of a damaged city.

All we want is to blubber our piece
from inside the blubbery belly of the beast.
All we want are some trees and a plot,
an updated bible – now look what we got.

It's no go, the East Side skaters.
Atlas on Fifth is supporting the globe.
It's no go, and the bishop and mayor
are smothered in their official robes.

It's no go, the campus body,
Union Square and the plebian hordes.
It's no go, at Washington Square
where the chessmen rule the outdoor boards.

The Knight is cantering over the squares
and the Rook is sweeping the black and the white.
The Queen reads poems in her boudoir
while the cowboy King is dying to fight.

You champagne rebels, eat your croissant.
Leek and hot-air is today's special quiche.
The king's bad-ass and big-time troops
are galloping out of your small-time reach.

All we want is a church or a stage.
The tickets are free – we're acting our age.
All we want is the voice of sweet reason.
Just asking the question, and we're guilty of treason.

It's no go, you Bowery bums,
you can drink to the passing muesli crowd.
The bishop, the firemen, candlestick-makers:
you're also no go, you're no allowed.

You better just face it, you ain't gonna go,
it's our UN – done dusted and barred.
You can chant and whine but the gate's still shut.
Wake up, get real, 'cause reality's hard.

It's no go, you marchers on Second
and no go, Fifth marchers and Seventh.
Stay put and sit on your goddamn ass
or we'll speed that ass into goddamn heaven.

It's no go, you raggle-tag protests.
Security means we'll be locking the chains,
doing our job to keep you alive
to weigh up the loss for the national gain.

All we want is to go but 'No go'
say all the policemen who are running the show.
All they say to our going's 'No go!
Go back to Soho and Dumbo...ho ho!'

All we want is to go, but 'No Go!'
say all of the newspapers and state radio.
All we say is: 'You stooges! Go blow!
We'll see in god's name who'll be running this show.'

NOTE: Barricades stopped thousands of protesters from attending the anti-war march in New York City on 15 February 2003.

To the Enemy

Sit down, have a chair and relax,
you who've made former friends bleed.
Here are all my questionable expenses
for the tax-man, the faithless to read.

Okay, so I drink, talk to strangers,
loudly befriending at parties
those lacking position, power or wealth,
who aren't distinguished or arty.

I slept with a man who was handsome
instead of the powerful editor
(not that I've ever claimed purer ethics –
it's just that I never knew better).

Please outline what's wrong with my life plan,
help map the route of my passions,
edit me into comfortable style
according to science or fashion.

It's not that I don't have ambition
or a liking for money or fame.
Is it just that I misinterpret the rules?
Don't I cheat well enough at the game?

Old Woman, Sentimental Song

Age cannot dim ya,
Yer a Lone Star pearl,
part of a necklace
wrapped round this world.

Yer age is a badge.
Wrinkles are fine.
Faces like clocks
show the accurate time.

M-O-U-R-and-N.
But tears stop and then
life starts again.
There's no tellin' when
M-O-U-R-and-N

Ye sure are darn old
but we love ya like that,
fer your supper fer one
and your can for the cat.

Yer photograph album
is golden with ages...
and weird stains and glue
and dead people's pages.

M-O-U-R-and-N.
But tears stop and then
life starts again.
There's no tellin' when.
M-O-U-R-and-N

Like the Grand Canyon
of history borne,
yer deep with experience,
monumentally worn

Age cannot dim ya,
Yer a Lone Star pearl,
part of a necklace
wrapped round this world.

M-O-U-R-and-N.
But tears stop and then
life starts again.
There's no tellin' when.
M-O-U-R-and-N.

The Bomb Aria

That one's called Wailer, and that one's Sheer Bliss.
You haven't lived till you listen to this.
Next on: the Great Granddaddy bomb.
To the end of your days you'll remember that shudder.

Like no other.

Now this one's the top of the list,
but its name is hard to remember.
Galaxy Cluster. That's it. Ace at dismembering.
This is my favourite, this track:
Screaming Hyena. High body count yield.

Takes me back.

And the final recording is Lilies of the Field.
Good for behind
the enemy lines
when there's nowhere to run.
Don't be fooled by a lyrical psalm,
a sweet melody like your girlfriend might hum.
You could search for this album for years.

Still moves me to tears.

from

THE ENGLISH EARTHQUAKE

The Refinery

You cannot look at narrow-brush moustaches.
You cannot think about gas-cookers, their ovens
flame-rimmed, the diadem of fire, or hear the bell
when it's done. Or think of teeth, lamp-shades, soap,
the refinery chimney-stacks, puffing cheerfully.

You cannot raise your hand in history class
to ask a simple question; your arm freezes
in a parody of salute. You cannot write 'horror'
because horror is a good film for anyone
with a strong stomach and a taste for gore.

Anyway, the antique photographs are grainy,
have blurred into art – that vaseline trick with the lens.

At dinner you sip the rot-gut wine
and listen to the table-talk – an operation botched
or an ache in the joints the doctor couldn't diagnose.
You choke with rage at the meal, gibbering,
while the devil samples your soul like buttered croissant.

Portholland

Fast-forward the years – this same inlet the little dipper
still filling, or tipping back its share; our converted chapel
salting up; the odd car's three-point turn. Old and parked

in our chairs, we find ourselves saying 'Tide's out again.'
Of course it is. Though now you're mostly worried by the divers
gone too long, diagonal gold fallen across the row of cottages

and a fire spreading on their Citroën windscreen, the cove
and its boulders swallowed whole by now. In the end, they emerge
but slowly, like a negative bloom: first, the twin black heads,

mouthless and goggled, then the black shoulders and torsos,
flippers last, until they stand there, streaming. They peel down
to sallow English flesh, boast about reserves of air.

Promising

The proverbial Englishman fondly knows his weather
like he knows his tea, makes his cocksure forecast
by wind-force, dubious light, some nebulous measure,
just as last night's overtaken lovers loved, star-kissed,

and told their innocent lies, meaning every thunderous word.
What is certain about brief rain, cloudy intervals
tongued by a hot sun, the contracts incurred
by unpredictability, those absolute integrals

of weather? Are we certain, lover, that we drive
this rain, or lightning, touching with our fingertips,
or does the timely dramatic flare just bribe
the future, glaze our eyes, while the ringing whips

of rain flail our promises into shape? Artful timpanist,
shots of alcohol light and we're fortune-tellers
paid by ourselves in gold, orchestrating the tempest
as if we'd seized control of Wotan's tiller.

The phone unrings, the bed remakes itself tonight;
if our fingers spark that next electric flash
and thunder still follows that instant of light
let's look down at our bare and promising flesh.

Power Games

The traffic eyes went blank with cataracts,
lorries buckled, the rigid aerial spines
bent for mutant coats – Uri Geller with a blank cheque.

The ant–column of cars wayward and drunk,
all the toy streets had wound down to crime
and accidents, the shops and offices funked.

At home, the TV sizzling like bacon,
we were rehearsing 'I love you' in pantomime –
difficult words for the practised pagan.

Think, that very day we juggled jump-lead cables,
bewildered by the dead car, those precarious lines
we were examining for plus and minus labels.

One false move, those red and blue aortas
could shock you the other side of "live", if misaligned –
the right key, the booby-trapped mortice.

We fell into the pub, sat comfortable in the dark
under currentless bulbs with lame plugs, sipping wine,
negotiating the odd, casual remark.

Then you broke the triangle with that effective
skilful shot; the white flew off the table
as all at once the mains switched on to that collective
'Ah', as if this were first light, the start of time.

Off Season

The Spanish waitresses are giggling at us
as they serve the coffee and bread, in a Benasque hotel
between seasons, when few tourists bother the town.
We laugh back, unsure, in our own language –
a marble reredos and mischievous misericords,
sacred and profane, strewn across the table;
the Pyrenees unmasked of snow. One girl takes this postcard boldly,
without asking, pretends to read the English;
another fingers the ragged hole in my sleeve
as if by right, the bit of flesh showing through; laughs.

Somehow we have advertised desire –
that tear perhaps, a tone overheard
and unmistakable in any language, the telling eyes.
Ringless hands allow them intimacy with ours, and the fact
that we shall never return to here, chances are.

Tonight we touch and it happens again,
the walls falling away. I can see them now,
the innocent girls in their kitchen
laughing and stripping for the imaginary skiers.
On TV a matador flourishes his cape, his pride
ridiculous, but, as always, sex is in the air he waves aside
as the crowd roars and he is falling too
with the wounds they have been aching for.

Hatred

You were dreaming of a witch with a withered arm,
the twin headlights of her vision yellowed and split.
She handed you twisted roots on a platter, laughed
and spoke in tongues – shrill backward words, mockery and spit.

Now she works her voodoo on your wax and cardboard
torso; you wake up in a freezing sweat, trying to cough
a weight from your chest, the moon's bulbous glare
exactly opposite, a dangling face with all the features wiped off.

Ode on St Cecilia's Day

Lights out, downstairs you wallow
in Wagner. Tossing in bed I swallow
philistine words: Turn off that blasted art.
It sometimes seems as if the cart
goes before the horse
when a soprano's voice
simulates some grand, transcendent part

of love we feel we should attain.
Formal court Baroque
never does the trick.
Far closer to the truth are those deranged
Beethoven late quartets that we both like.
And real-life unreels in your brain

as you listen to Mahler – suffering refrains
and marches. A childish tune, warped, sustains
that later piercing note
before finally some hope
or resignation in the ending reigns.

Love's intensified while the music plays –
before too long
we sing 'our song' –
and symphonies repeat the misery-phrase
or even found that phrase for all our loving days,
for when they're gone.

Coffee

Alley cats howled about love
outside, besotted terrible strains

as we swallowed it cup by cup
like pain, drop after measured drop

in our cave-like kitchen, smelled that rotten
exotic wood, heard the water sob,

dribble down, hiss and steam.
We filled the empty jugs with night,

coffee, the swirling oils,
threw the sodden filter away

with the dregs, the slag-heap horrors
and started all over again;

clean water drenched the grains
to a peaty, impacted mass

and again we tasted the bitterness,
poured milk and sugar into the black.

Forcing Flowers

We are naming hybrids. The next one's
Bastard. It's still possible to make
these new strains up. All the fun's
gone however. You too would like to break me
into what I'm not. We're learning zero
but that things are getting worse, from this
astounding failure to another. Love's missed
because we knew it once. We lie to retrieve it,
hopelessly, with letters and with photos,
pain outweighing pleasure, and still believe,
sure it's not the memory that pinks
it into flower. Leaning over, the erstwhile hero
delicately sniffs: memory *is* a rose.
Now, we keep hothouses. In them everything stinks.

Spells

A curse on the lover with shyness as plausible cover for his black
    lies.
A curse on his leather furniture sticking to the skin.
A curse on his row after row of tasteful jazz
and the glass table's cutting edges.

A blessing on my cobalt blue vase
and a spray of lemon fuchsia, and forgetting.

A curse on 4 a.m., the light like soot or burnt milk in a pan.
A blessing on the dawn and dusk, when the sun and moon are large and
    shimmering.

A curse on the memories like storm clouds in my heart.
A blessing on the storm clouds outside my window.
A curse on the useless letters I never throw away.
A blessing on my right arm for its sharp delivery.
A curse on my sharp tongue for its sharp delivery.

A blessing on the Lyric muse when she is kind to me.
A curse on the Lyric muse, for she is on holiday in the Bahamas.
A blessing on the warm salt seas for their constancy and power.
A curse on the razor-clams slicing bare feet.

A blessing on foreign countries: their birds and trees, their people, their
    clothing, their houses and songs.
A curse on their wars, our wars.
A blessing on their dawn, their dusk, their seas, even their deceitful men.
A blessing.

Lunar Eclipse

While scientists are asleep
we are taking the moon in
for our purposes. Our shadows creep

across the disc, like curtains,
but so slow, we can hardly guess
until its staring certain

light suffuses to a reddish, tissue glow,
more like what we often hope to see:
the astronomy of the soul.

Belial

My neighbours have given birth to a monster
I regret to say. His moon-like pate
glows in the dark like a diabolical nite-lite.
He cuts his milk-teeth on steel, and shrieks
the kind of shrieks which can stop your heart. Literally.
He shits mountains in every room. Moves them too.

Isn't he adorable, croon the harpies from down the block.
Cootchie-coo. He sucks their wrinkled fingers dry.

His parents sleep with him in his Alien-papered room
because they are under his thumb
which is as big as the Goodyear blimp.
But when mummy and daddy *have* to go out,
sorrowfully and lovingly, they fasten his furry handcuffs
and wrap him in his terry-cloth straitjacket
which is blue for boys. He bites his mother good-bye.

Then it's time to chew his play-plax, build Trump towers
and Hefner swimming pools, or DNA with a frightful twist.

Getting home too late that night,
his parents hear him bawl the theme of *Neighbours*
from a block away. They better hurry up.
The sitter should have been home hours ago.

Eden

These are lukewarm days.
Even a murder would be better.

All the birds are fussing
about love, and flowers threaten
to bloom. That gingerbread
home I could eat with greed.
Too sweet to live in!

Love is also too sweet.
There's all that schmaltzy music
played with love and nature.
Who on earth's directing this?

O bring me religion and strife!
I cannot go on like this.

Trompe l'œil

The architrave is classical, the ruins
necessarily distant, drawn from life.

On the trumeau, between the window
and non-window, goes a watercolour,

runny and vague, of a river and old mill.
We must people its banks, have good views.

The mill-owner, watching us, is dead and history
when we turn away. Look what art can do:

marry urban surreal to greenery, the nature
in art being what you choose. Green belongs

on walls, and windows needn't be true.
I am not *deceived* by this picture

of outside and I am not deceiving
anyone in my mansion on the river.

Grand plans! If you lack symmetry or scenery
(and you have the time) paint a window

to look like a window. Make wild art.
But also make your framework strong.

What could be missed are the darkened,
sweaty faces just around the corner, advancing.

A fool says: *Pay to wipe the murder
off their faces. They are real.*

The English Earthquake

Somewhere, a cup tinkles in its saucer.
A meek 'oh my' passes down the miles
of manicured gardens, as armies rumble

the monuments of cities continents away.
The budgie chirps 'goodness' to thin air
while Bach quivers slightly and the fat roast

sways in the oven, brain-dead, but chuckling
in its oil. Such a surprise: the settling ground,
innocent with rape and mustard, groaning

under its weight of roses. The premier
sees stars, plumps her pillows for photographs.
Alas, *Watchtower* faces are falling as life goes on

and the Ex-Major winds back years to the war –
its incendiary thrill – his wife flushed
with disbelief as the earth moves unexpectedly,

the giant baby at the core of the planet
rocking its apocalyptic cradle
gently, wailing: 'Hungry, hungry, hungry.'

Brooklyn Bridge

(designed by Roebling and finished by his daughter-in-law Emily)

This one's mine: not a nail-less Bridge of Sighs
nor a stage, where enemies or film crews shoot
but trembling on a net of 'wheres' and 'whys',
part Asses' Bridge, part Al-Sirat, less Iron Brute,

more hunkering church: grown from Gothic grey
with its cables spun from spiders bred in books.
That dark harp was made for me to play.
And however dark, I couldn't help but look

at ever darker slights, their height and girth
stringing me high above the traffic's hum.
I was harnessed by a yoke of fear, from birth,
less myself while adding to that sum –

the way the architect's now ailing daughter
laid her father's body, right across the water

Time Out

Imagine there being no exacting word for time,
there being nothing to waste or save, invent
or slip away. Then who would fight the crime
of its fast passing? I'd take, say, the three-cigarette

train departing half-past-after-the-last-word
which wants saying – and not a moment too soon! –
while the numberless dial of my watch would refer
to a changing mise-en-scène winding from sun to moon,

or some event to an eventual end, when a black 'For Hire'
drives me home on its own good time. *Good* time. For tides
aren't for living by, but are only there to admire
occasionally on trips to the timeless seasides.

Nor do we milk cows, farm a natural time, say to friends:
'I'll meet you at the end of this cooking of rice'
or, more vaguely still: 'You know…when the afternoon ends'.
When? Would I be on time, guided by a smoky feel of night,

when it fell, in my bones – another made-up clocking-in machine?
But how would I measure these purposeful distances run,
or almost run, as the case would more likely seem?
The racers might just laugh or chat at the starting-gun.

Some joke, infernal time! Not a word, not well-made policy,
but some black jester's dressed-up devastating game
which lets me put off the proverbial plot, infinitely,
so I could wait here forever before you finally came, or not.

Homesteading

It was official, in an American sort of way,
that the weather was obedient
as a dog on a leash
heeling close to each new settlement.

Ella Spawn was content for fourteen months
before she sold up for a café future in Williston.
Thereafter, Rush Blankenship takes up her written tale:
a line or two of marriage, and retail stock.
Beecher Leach of North Dakota,
remaining unmarried his entire life,
is yet remembered by some for his fried bread doughs.

See the bladeless windmill
stubbornly at attention in the hot wind
near cottonwoods ringing an empty space,
the corral's modernist geometry of sinking lines.

The buffalo wealth up the chimney for good,
now it's buffalo westerns keep you warm.

There in the central plains, one Dr Vernon
(later kicked upstairs into government)
crossed his pale white arm
over thousands of square miles, in a flash,
pronouncing them fair: *Rain follows the plow.*
The cloth got pulled out once the tables were set.

What of Thorstien Odden with his Hardanger violin?
What of Gilbert Funkhouser, that jokester?
Wherefore Stella Swab and Oliver Fedge?

Some choked on meat, coughed one too many times
or ditched the prairies for the North or East,
anywhere of a greener or colder complexion.

And, well, no damper in your stove pipe
is as good a fame as any, mark this,
or death in a flax bin,
or even a novel method of shocking the grain.

Victorine Berquist had the last word.
To visit neighbours, then up and walk away!
No sign to her shack she'd ever thought to leave.
No sign of her was ever found.
Just a whole continent, big as this paragraph.

Sin

A flash pool-game, some freak hormonal wiring,
the cab-ride where he gets my drunken yes
and I'm rooked in that dump of a hotel on Forty-Eighth,
that naked room – no secrets but the big one –
with blunt razors studded round a scummy bath,
a dusty portable, no printed matter anywhere,
just a few chairs knifed with the dead initials
of those who went too far, or never far enough.

Station-waiting

The conductor's whistle dies,
this time not for me:
another train easing off from between
the grey-slate platforms. Trains go gently
over fields, at first so slowly
deepening into the woods, their damage
vague, cumulative.
But trains make gladness blossom in me
sudden and hard
when I watch them pass. Aboard
it is another thing, of course.

I wait on a bench, holding
a paper chosen for its easy-
to-turn pages, simple headlines lying
crossways, letters deceptively large,
a box of matches too in hand, on it
a printed swan sailing forth, and far
above my head the sky-
light illusion.

From here it seems
the tracks snake into knots,
bonding for brief lengths,
then dividing, re-meeting further down
the line – I wait, I pace.
My train will leave from here
for some direction, rifle
through countryside, the land
unrolling violently, months
unreeling finally. I imagine
a child's coin placed on the rails.
Quickly, the carriage wheels tick over
and it flattens and loses its shine
but once the face is erased,
some elements gleam again. Leave-taking

should be swift, a flinging
of self into a great blankness and behind
the screen-door of a lit-porch slams shut. The shock
of that bang should hurry you along.

I fold the paper in quarters
and the newsprint dyes my fingers black,
words lightening imperceptibly;
its newness smells of chemical.
In an hour I'll throw it away.
The blood-tipped matches come closely crowded.
Only a few will fail; only a few will light.

Ending up in Kent

I'm leaning out the cottage window, latch
unfastened, trying to see for miles, further.
Postcard-picture me in a country of thatch,
twisted lanes, daub and wattle. I entertain
with coal-fires and gas cylinders.
For all through the year it rains, I freeze.
The neighbouring oasts are like spindles,
fat with the wound-up thread of absent summer.
I walk detergent streams, in search of trees.

Someone's put me in a story-book, but kills
every tree before my entrance.
I follow an ordnance map and find
frightening rows of straight and vacant pines.
The earth as barren as the rugs
people in my nearby town put down. Medicine
sting of pine. Listen there, hear nothing. No bird sings.
I'm told that insects are the only living things
in that Forestry Commission flat. And slugs.

Gala-day on the Tonbridge-Hastings line
and my landlord's chopping down his chestnut trees.
Two train stops and you're at a famous waters place
where they renovate shops into sepia prints.
Inside are offices, outside a show of wealth. In me,
when I walk that scenic, cobbled walk, a tall tree
grows crooked, like a money-graph
zigzagging into civic failure. In warm weather
they sell sulphur from the wells for your pleasure.
Good Health! November and the Guy will burn.
What leaves are left on what trees are left will turn.

Where I Live

This is my rinkidink town where the galleon down by the pier
swings on its monstrous hinge, higher and higher
above the Parade and the Palace, the face-lifted Grand,
where the toy bombs went pop and out came the hankies,
the sweet violins: but its front – zipped back up again pronto,
creamy, deluxe – is riddled with elegant spy-holes
where the powerful stare down the sea to a pin-point
rendering it harmless, a piss in a bucket.

On the tarted-up boardwalk, videos sweat and contest
for their sitting-duck targets, after the lights have gone out
finally, late, very late in the night, when the clairvoyant's
left with her ultimate line of deceit; her fatalist streak
has followed her home where the silvery ropes of the slugs
knot infinities over her carpet, trails of the money
she's palmed from the tourists whose luck had already run out.

Bang your spade against your bucket:
Where does anger bed down for the night?
The dolphins go round in their underground circles
of fever, then die. We squat on the shingle

and bang our spades against our buckets,
the westernmost pier now shorn of its land-loving arm,
just like that, not by freak winds or overblown tides.
We're taking our chances elsewhere. The stilts sag down softly
to splayed-out position, punt weakly away from the shore
and the island drifts out to sea. Indifferently.

Dens Road Market

It's a pity that Dante could not be brought back and compelled to live in Dundee for a little; he would add a sensational new circle to his Inferno.
HUGH MACDIARMID

Key of the door,
two and one: twenty-one
and we're through to the musty
indoor market smell, its tobacco and spit

and yellowed decor,
the outdated goods, and the otherworldly drone
of the bingo caller, presiding unjustly
at her horse-shoe counter, where the housewives tick

their lucky sevens
on damp cards. We browse through Book Club trash
and Pat Boone cassettes – the bindled rooms
of scarves and skirts, unstrung rackets, laceless shoes,

the traders in heaven
I guess, or possibly at grass,
their vacant booths like ragged, burlapped tombs
in rows, instead of the usual *Back at Two*s.

Unlucky for some,
one and three. Blind Thirty.

Where's the fun
in that caller's drab and deadened certainty,
her business of numbers, the surprise grave
for that headless Barbi doll I lost? *Kelly's eye, on its own,*

Number One.
O Genie of the five-and-dime, the bargain basement's dirty
cellars, where the thrifty dead can save,
who put all my stuff in this stall? *Here is wisdom.*

114

That no man might buy or sell,
save he that had the mark or name of the beast
(clickety-click,
six-hundred three score at least)

or the number of his name. Well.
I scram with the cry of 'House' at my back.

Distancing in Wales

The clouds have abandoned the earth
to its clarity of rowan berry and heather flower
as if to go away is to elucidate,
learn what we mean by each unloosening hour.

After ribbons of track and trees and macadam,
after the deadening service-station miles,
the sheep seem placed on hills by your warm hand
resting near the inscrutable telephone dial.

The wild bracken, brilliant gorse, the perpetual wind
ruffling that lake of undergrowth
all say 'Forget; your windy life, desires
aren't worth a half a length of rope.'

But love links miles like a telephone,
that ripened silence driven down bad wires,
and the abandoned mines, the estuary
could come into life through art, or artless fire.

Or forget archaic riches, the idiomatic sheep,
this language evaporating like steam,
all the place names where you are not;
what they possibly, to me, could mean.

The kite shifts valleys, the relentless river
pours out a song we seem to understand
until one day the language dries up altogether
and we must learn to speak in other lands.

Running Away from Home

Do stations make you want to run somewhere –
skip out, tear up your fortunes,
your lot? Your errand is delivery. A luckier one

boards a train, but you aren't going any place
standing there. Trembling with pioneer spirit
you say goodbye to the leavers and kick off home.

'I want! I want!' burns itself on a pyre,
private countries of people passing you by.
Who could ever cross those borders anyway?

The traffic is humming with wishes,
and you want to steer from your outdated
destiny, into another. But thank god

life is thrilling constantly somewhere better
than you will ever be. Does it make you want, or want
to want to fly – that jet roar – distant as stars,

passing you over? The trains, the giant planes:
they make you ache to be going. What about the birds
flying, dolphins swimming, the wild animals running

a pot-boiler version of glory you can't shake off –
running from hunters, that great adventure of death,
back to the safety of their known and wild woods?

Air Mail

Words travel badly.
Unwieldy and hard to fold
into smaller bundles,
they take up far more space
than the grain of their truth would occupy.
Those launched over the ocean to you
careen wildly, collide with other letters,
or return to sender,

packages mauled, shredded and torn into strips.
Few arrive intact.
As a battleground for love, the Atlantic
is too enormous and too romantic-sounding
for the bad language. Daggers rust,
fall useless into the sea.

Take the words: *I love you.*
Disembodied, though tantalising,
they arrive at your hearing.
Anybody might have sent them
to the wrong address.
Or: *I ache for you.*
The *ache* has journeyed long distances,
is tired with itself.
How does one ache for a *you*?
What is a *you* and where?
Take these words: *You do not understand.*

Print them and post them back.
We are just our words.

from

BARGAIN WITH THE WATCHMAN

QUOGUE REFUGE
(for Van)

Sexual Love

The motorboat's charge
trickles to shore, diminishing.
The bay tends back towards peace.

And that's why I like it;
though clamming by foot takes time,
a certain readjustment of the will.

At first, the mud's unwearable
for its soft give, the deepening
silent rip of ancient silk:

the way it clings around the ankles,
will never tear, or tears
repeatedly, the old healing.

Pilgrim

The beach was a shrine of steel in summer.
Its muscular heat stunned me face-down in prayer,

devotions buried in the scallop-shelled sand.
I was the shocked one, unable to faint

and impress the oak-smoked boys, the lavender girls
who just stepped over me with the meanest care.

How I kissed the shore of my shame and wishing!
And eternity rushed to meet them in a wave.

Anschluss

(in memory of Samuel & Frances K. Salzman)

We summered in the lap of Peconic Creek,
one of the thousand warm cloisters in the bay.

Low tide slung out its most generous shore,
peppered with the breath-holes of softshell clams,

clumps of mussels knotted deep in the reeds.
But the neighbours opposite, in a smooth finesse,

deal themselves the acres we thought to own:
our marsh rewritten into the flawless sand

of Pine Neck, where new money grows gold potatoes
and folds the fields, like egg-white, into condominiums.

Their sleek pine dock has stilts, fresh as breadsticks,
thin and snappable; chiffon floats out from motorboats.

We yaw in their wake, thumping the waves. An oar
divides the seaweed as we row hard, just to stay still.

Grandmother

The bay's little waves licked the ankles
as her poled net loitered through the warm shallows,
seaweed caught and weeping from its bent rim
Home again, ripples from the pail told the story.

When she rolled her trousers above her aged knees,
you knew where she was headed-across the milkweed field,
into the pines, past a single cactus and the oval frame
of massed catkins, to reach the wide open bay of pure joy.

Cross Out

They must have known that we escaped – if only
by some slight shade across their dreams –
how our cunningly angled steps bluffed the old staircase
from its customary whinge. Then, to be home free,

we'd only have to slow the screen-door's bite,
slipping into the crickets' deafening pitch
to take the first sprint through the pines which night
unified into something we'd hardly dare enter, but did

until we'd break through the boundary of parenthood
to where the moon held itself over the marshes
patiently, unnoticed by us now released into noise
and racing down the beach towards the boys.

Natural Habitats

A house for summer only, still its stubborn damp
outlasted August, sand lining the sheets;
though visitors practically rhymed their praises
over marasmius, boletus, cherrystone clams.

A panic of bees tucked itself into the eaves,
belonged, earning a season's grace. In the shade
father made himself busy with important papers,
his monster of a typewriter bucking and heaving.

Ace birder, he knighted himself with a nom de plume
– acres and acres to be overseen and written up by noon –
while mother spaced on shelves her rows of silenced jars:
the essential sugars of blueberries, beach-plums.

Snug in the hot berth of my bedroom, I cribbed for love
and studiously plucked my eyebrows into surprise –
candy and movie-magazines strewn across the covers.
They could never imagine what I was thinking of.

Boreal Owl

You could call it an outing, father-style:
driving the two night hours, hard on the single-white,
to that Connecticut wood, crowded already
with twitchers – the misguided, the obsessed.

Don't get me wrong. I like nature.
But I froze for ages slimmed behind
my chosen tree, the owl's fabled panoramic scan
failing to oblige the pencil-tickers.
When the head did turn, heavily indifferent,
he had to admit it was the common variety.
There were too many witnesses.
You can't complain. These are the risks.

Lucky Strikes

Her father was smoking fortune's cigarettes
in those gondola days. Golden boy. Teacher's pet.
Though he had far too many areas of expertise.
Chances are *he* found the morels, dismissed the lesser trees
she found beautiful, identified the tiny bird on the furthest branch.
Then there was the oyster ritual – the salt-water brooks
running into the sink, a childish lop-sided set of the mouth
as he jimmied a blunt knife into the weakest part of the hinge.

It changes, doesn't it; the Châteauneuf becomes a binge
alone, at night, as he fingers the leaves of someone else's books
after the actress's brush-off, the failed business-lunch.
All his minuscule reputations will retire, migrate south
to homes in Florida, where the girls are less amazing, less amazed
and his bird-counts lengthen into the darkening glade.

Quogue Refuge

Only the sick can be caged
without a moral dilemma.
Yet here was a child's delight:
a hunched American eagle,
a dulled racoon,
the Barn Owl continuing to measure
the girth of our planet.

We had come once more to compass
the pond's perimeter.
We were the very charge in our circuit!
Horseflies butted the air.
The fields were rancid with milkweed.
Soon Maple Swamp would redden
its fluttering rags to a bull.

And did I not learn to love
the wildest things, out of habit,
dragging my adolescent weight,
impatient at Father Time
who never caught up with his binoculars?

There I stood,
bored at the back of beyond,
with a chance to break the set
and yet failing to twig,
having valued myself so long in imprisonment.

Memorable

From the window of Mary's rancho house,
we could just take in the risk, the stillness
loading the summer resort, see down Fairline Drive's
repeating tic-tac-toe of x-marked glass
like hysterical fun, imagining Dune Road's docks
tilting all these years towards danger,
dreamy lobster boats bobbing at their tethered station
as the swell tries its force against the jetty.

But put aside the thought of dead and swollen animals
floating like bathtub toys, the weatherboard
ripped from country cottages, the flying cars
or the masterpiece of a newly-broken inlet;
that was 1938, impacted into your local guide,
someone else's thrill, a better tale, and true.

The Pine Barrens

That burnt forest is no accident
around those dwarf-plain parts,
that spine of glacial moraine,
debris of vast and ancient
slow-as-tortoise waves of ice.
The trick's to love and praise
twisted, blackened flagpoles
shorn of fluttering flags,
the scrubby undergrowth
and all the dregs left over

once pine-cones burst their seeds
in a crack of blistering heat.
There, to light a cigarette
might be to generate unplanned
– think of that – and also die.
I remember lying sprawled
across a rippling, shifting
golden lake of light, spread
across your snow-white coverlet.

Even then I measured loss,
all the many drowning pleasures,
remembered in advance to mark
the shortest page of happiness
for much later, a little later too,
for strolling out among the hosts
of whole and solid people
walking with a special ease

in a studied, casual parade
downtown, of nearly Spanish cheer.
What a marvel, the managed lives,
their deft and inadvertent slide
into the manufacturing business:
the production, start to finish
of whole and solid people

you could almost put your fist through.
I had to make the tourists vanish
even if they left more space
than I could ever use, or ever fill.
Then fall came, winter, round
and round again, and us now far

from stunted pines, though the bony roots
poke the ground inside of me.
I've rated every season, certain now
fall pools deepest, deepest down.
Its wild motif draws up the ash

and that day's flash of sun on maple.
Fall empties me, and I sinned by loving
emptiness, the god-like powers
of imagining, and god-like pain.

In spring again, in Christian lands
I think: one son's one more than none.
It seems impossible each time, nothing

will come of this – unholy even –
or ever will, you say in bed

one day; I blow my smoke into the air.

Phantoms

I should not look for you
where the tide drains out of the marsh,
but under the hidden tufts of grass
where it floods in.
Though there's little chance of tracking down
nature's secrets, still, I follow this walk,
the leak into the ebbing pond
where the fat pipe sucks moisture
out of the lowlands,
follow the pull through the neck
of the body of water into the currents of bay.
Does that boat pull away the tide?
Does it drag its wake like a fish-catch
or like an enormous anchor of which
it is always trying to be free?
Who drives the motor out of the harbour?
No one to tell me; it has vanished now into the sea.

A blue heron beats slowly out of the rushes
and heavily circles the mud-banks
risen up shining at their lowest hour.
He dives and misses his food;
I turn and go home.
Another day, a dream of you moves me outside to find
the answer it nearly gifted me with,
drives me down the twisted pine-needled path,
its white sand salmon-tinted in the sunset.
A strange light glances off the trees,
hovering just beyond the next leaves.
Behind, the screen door flaps, its poor voice retreats
and the pale house falls into the cover of woods.
I push open the woven reeds that cut,
slosh over the wetlands,
and suddenly stop
half-way through a breath on the desert shore.

Painting by Numbers

Now that the pursed orange kisses
of the trumpet-flower
have troubled the old walls enough,

the oak has broken the hammock twice,
the mushrooms have rearranged themselves
too many autumns in the same field,

something gives; tiny drops lightly sizzle
and a million leaves tremble and dip.

So I double-lock front and back,
wandering through each sandy room

– the hook-weave rugs damp and gritty,
the glass globes of insect cemeteries filling up –

to where the parlour's organ stops are frozen
in confusion: some Bach fugue
or just the whim of children.

Here hangs *his* version: our garage, but vineless,
young, its wide doors painted open

to a new Ford, a kerosene lamp lit
forty years back, before the haze
stole over his oils, distance blurred by trees,

before this thunder lolloping over
our pale and elemental house

crashes through the weatherboard
and finds me with the dog beneath the bed.

Seamother

The black conch reconnects
the plaintive distance: '*Seamother?*

There's nobody here by that name.'
Only afterwards, holding on, I wonder

and miss the loose, smooth dunes
of the East Coast, its ice-age legacy

of pestled sand hotting up
to an agate-bruised shore,

the gauze tides conjuring summer
from the salted wood of stilts and quays

when a dark-green thrill upends me
and iodine rushes into my mouth.

I imagine him re-dial, coolly,
surer than I of a clear line through.

Here, shoals crackle, the undertows hiss
since the grain's not fine enough to burn.

Neither can the slow and gentle manatee,
sadly, be reached at this number,

her mermaid rumours docked,
the temporal spell resumed

though I grip the receiver,
making my calls.

Childish

I'm swimming in a cartoon,
lazily, under a smiley sun.
Sails, stitched with chunks of colour,
zig-zag into the frame and out
as outboards blubber a happy song.

Now enter a daytime moon
the criss-cross waves have spun
which floats around my shoulders.
No one I know is about
when suddenly there chugs along

our chubby-faced, old-style saloon.
Uh oh goes the little hand-brake,
and out steps real life.

Case History

Five-years-old, backed against a wall
shielding spring from L'École Rousseau
and the paved yard endured at recess,
she's a wooden Babushka, painted shut
in a hail of stones. And who can say
that that tiniest doll, the deepest version
weighty as lead, wasn't born fully-formed?

Children loop and veer, their after-images
tangled in furious games of tag,
the knot they tied still tightening.
Or were they her friends, just one bully
ferried to France and handed his rock
by a future grievance? (A further unwinding
would even reveal the doctor at her birth
delivering her with inauthentic love.)

So. Next door, she orchestrates maypoles
fountaining ribbons, a view of harmonious
pastelled girls, whose luck runs in circles,
the sundial leaning towards the golden hour
as they float inside, invisibly cued.
The tears are drawn to remind, not soothe.
It may *not* have happened like this. It's possible.

Physics

I'm skiving off again, this time pasting down old family photographs
in strict chronology, with tacky titles (the wasters' trick
I could call work, of ordering a mess in retrospect
to make it count) when I find my grandfather at thirty-six

and picture him, still earlier, clinging to his mother,
who, in turn, has him slung around her neck – a tin-type in a locket –
as they pass through Ellis Island where their bones are checked,
stale bread criminally stuffed in their unfashionable pockets.

There's bread here too. And his son, my father, has popped up
fully-formed in the Natural History Museum cafeteria
with its futuristic, stark formica, the cutlery magnetised
in wild patterns the waitress only dreams about, the interior

like a spaceship, and both looking used to travelling in time.
Though now, at ninety, his love of science is reduced to cranky bursts:
'Cripes, what's the point of everything?' he gruffly asks the air
as his rucked arm encompasses the dumbness of the universe

– words which tell me all I ever want to know about growing old.
So it's odd, this little astral-plane vignette; between the two
a möbius strip unfurls the constancy of the lunch ever to come,
the bread he always ate with every meal untouched, waiting like a clue

on the spartan counter – a planetary jumble of rolls
in a basket, and glimpsed behind the glass of undrunk water
a giant thumb; father and son half-turned in their chairs
expecting momentarily the prodigal daughter.

Poor Relations

1

This is your heart, a lump of quartz
with just a hint of amethyst.

Read the finished auction list.
Remove the Tokyo imports.

2

Your suffering is performance, and deserves a fee.
Let's open this Vaudeville nativity
in the upstate New York town of Bethlehem
– near to Auschwitz, Athens, Rome, Manoa –
where you agonised on a velvet ottoman,
ashamed of falsity – your feather boa,
your very genes of braided coral, the diadem,
You could have refused to go on!

Theatre modernised the witch's wand,
her gift of thirty-seven dollars banked
as standard rite of passage in the western world.
She spat in an elegant lacy handkerchief
pinched your cheeks to rose, bleached you blonde,
then had you waltzing for her prime antiques.
Most precious are these hardest words of thanks
to the woman who has costed all desire.

3

Free the floating souls from her paperweights.
Smash the Staffordshire lover's curls
and smash the strings on his muse's lyre.

Everywhere lies evidence – a missing limb
on the French rococo cherubim,
an empty place among the lapis horde.

Now behead the Celtic prince,
unmanned already without his sword.

Ah. This sounds authentic. A violent tryst.
There must be something in this
and in the curios like pearly hand-grenades
along the wall...

4

You told her how you died each tutu pasquinade.
St Vitus! St Genesius!
All the hollow-plaster saints!

Images in thrall
to the mirror's Aphrodite crest.

There were kisses like opals, crazed.
The kiss of her old age.

Which means you must forgive her all,
transpose each piece of wealth.

Applause like sleet
ticks on the wood of winter trees.
The lights go down. Finis.
You're feeling sorry for yourself.

5

This is the pencil scar
hallmarked in the palm of the hand –
the heraldic shield for the sisters of war.

If your sister couldn't dance, couldn't sing
and might as well have been nothing,
she'd take what jewels she could wear
to make the inheritance fair.

All women will be asked to stand
to be judged by diamonds and looks,
bodily wit and silver plate,
to prove how you're bound to reiterate
the greed and fury already long planned.

There are no true gods for these reference books,
only mortal indices of precious stones,
French paste, cut steel and mourning pieces,
stocks and bonds and sub-let leases,
private schools, Art Deco fans,
all picked up at bargain rates.

One Grand Tour each to the Holy Land
in search of more authentic roots.

When you measure your gloves against her boots,
the disputed satin gown
which the servant ends up taking down,
you find you share a marbled spleen,
specially designed. You who thrive on loans
and privileges! The moths in wool
eating more, became less full.

Your sister is your enemy.
Each day you scythe through her memory
to clear the field for enmity.
So much for the golden age, this is the golden plan.

6

How to extricate the bitterness from jet
and tell the story from its artificial set.
Blood was a satin ribbon on the quilted bedding.
Here's rage drawn delicate in marquetry,
the milky vases with bisque flowers at their mouths
like petrified condolences
made more valuable as elements.
Someone's breath, captured in Venetian glass.
The blistered lemon bowl
was cut for geomancy
and not for punch or profiteroles.

The mind's in shotgun wedding
with the object of its fancy
– no lack of ardour, be assured.
Now judge that stoneware's class!
Trash that imitation shepherd/shepherdess amour!

7

This has a religious cast,
his cock at half-mast
as he begins to arrange the scene in his head.
I'm reluctant to be naked on the bed.
Use it. *A convenient resistance.*
The bargain struck at his insistence.
It's good. Dark. Metaphysical. Am-Dram
has me squirming like the victim I really am
or intend to be.

Watch a woman come amazingly.
Well-hung with his bronze artefact,
he's done it. That last and best male task.
Now he can relax.

Surrender cannot be coerced,
though the broker's well-versed,
a stickler for technique and articulate wooing.

We both of us were salesmen, each with plans
but different currencies in hand.
Desire calculates its own undoing.

8

There is a jewel, Tiana Beach,
its agate pools just out of reach.

The sand across his skin
was buried when the tide came in.

His legs were bridges, strong and narrow.
I longed to lie beneath their shadow.

Blinding lustre! Then we lay down
on the forest's gold medallion.

The glory-hole was dripping glass.
Our island souvenir was cast.

Yet I never quite identified
the colour of his bedroom eyes.

The sand across his skin
was buried when the tide came in.

The fig-tree leaf was just a laugh.
I didn't know the joke by half.

The sand across his skin
was buried when the tide came in.

The moon played topaz tricks
in the form of an eclipse.

More fool me, that I reject
what was a genuine effect.

There must be catalogues, reserves
set at limits we deserve.

The sand across his skin
was buried when the tide came in.

9

Witness now the amateur's most obvious mistake
of lavishing an extra coat upon a masterpiece,
the so-called patient brush – heroic or discourteous.

Oh god, I am a fake!

I am gold in its most pure form,
too soft to hold a weight of fear.
Alloy is the answer here.

10

The satyr mustard-pot was never silver, the inkwell
never plate but worthless. So she sold them cheap.
Then of course they both change into platinum.
That was the luck a thousand charms dispelled.

11

You're the Queen of Misrule,
with a false pass through the fan-light portal
and into the penates vestibule

where Ethel, Gertrude, Ben are neatly hanging, so calm
and professional at playing mortal,
posed in the wedding or funeral stance.

Drink the sherry of melted carnival glass.
A toast to devalued heredity.
A wild dance.

12

Now that she's gone you can drink from Diogenes cup,
drink from those alabaster palms,
that priceless Art Deco kitsch
always held clear of your grubby kid grip.

Now that she's sound asleep
you find yourself loving imperfect items:
broken, unsaleably worn, of little worth,

washed-out jade, foxed ivory and horn,
old lamps with nothing to light them,

the astrological junk-heap
of Saturn's iron rings, a novelty Earth
disfigured with porcelain cysts,
outdated facsimile maps
and cosmetically altered angels, undone,
revealed in their true condition
– islands of amber glue on their wings
and fractured wrists –

as daylight splits the velvet gloom,
illuminating the family rooms.

The only things you can love
must be beyond repair.

The ceiling rose's plaster
is flaking grey snow in your hair,

the finials' dry husk of leaves firmly ground
to dust as soft as an old woman's skin.

13

The Queen of Misrule transmutes to an ass
on wheels, threadbare and rusty and browned,
jammed into the corner, unable to move,

as the numbers cascading from the face
of the backward grandmother clock,
faster and faster,
are swiftly, invariably replaced,
branded in from behind
like a Tiffany ornament signed.

You've shrunk, doll-size, to a miniature land
where *adorable* terrifies in the author's hands.

Air, water and grave.
What else can be saved

now you're tagged and buried in taffeta chaos
as the vaulting lurches and lowers,
closing your case.

Locked in! With only yourself to consider or break!
A decade of silence
containing the violence.
And just when you think it will never be over,
the cool air hits like a wave.

Somebody lifts you up by the neck,
hands you down.

Page One

As if a seam savagely rips open mid-60s, Brooklyn, New York,
I sit up on my top bunk to clock the golden sheet of light
slipped ritually beneath our closed door
and shadowed with a sketchy text
of figures coming and going

in the parental sacrament: beyond the time of goodnights,
when the piano's four hands bridge upwards to form
a rest which stretches past silence, begging
the question about that next note
ever getting played at all.

Then, as now, my double sleeping below, I'd have to lean out
dangerously, to launch a word into that midnight crossing.
At eight, we're connoisseurs of painted breasts,
psychedelica, the scent of weed, patchouli,
the charm and grit of our tooth fairy.

To the left, at the empty desks' twin dark-red forms no scholars sit
but empty people flattened in cartoon faints, the missing's
dresses slumped on chair backs, the static-laden
tights dangling above the pigeon-toed shoes
frozen in a first small step.

I draw back my tiny, doll-like curtains, to expose the dirty collage
of panes, to feel my body underground as the very root
of itself, to check my revolving door on history:
I burn next door's house each night,
I choreograph feral cats. Eye-

level, they slip among massed weed and jagged pavement tombstones
thrust up at crazy angles – the global earthquake damage
caused by something deep inside of us I guessed,
and the job of night: the job of us all.
We must be inside out,

next door nothing but seared girders, a final spark of embers arcing
into thread to bind charred ribs. One beam breaks and tumbles,
pounds the ground with future punctuation. Either that
or this: we've turned it outside in, palaces rebuilt,
grey shingle resuming the shape

of that house of two spinsters. One's still shrieking down a string
of yards; the other immutably sane. On that my curtains shut
to sharpen darkness, the thin knife of light slicing through
the bottom of my door, the knife
now, in my hand.

Flight of Books

His talk ranged over Bach and Socrates
and there was little I could add or say
since conversation with him went one way.
But, hey, so it is with all big cheeses.

All four of us at meals had books installed
upright, before our plates – hovering vultures
eyeing up our upper-case 'C' Culture.
Our silences turned summer turned into fall

when dining at my table, at my shoulder,
someone else must tell me what I think.
No one's qualified, now that I'm older.
Just me and my oration fuelled by drink.
Just me releasing birds from the child's folders
so they fly their flight. Or swim. Or sink.

Christmas at the In-Laws

The photos showed how they were bored: frozen poses
denoting pleasure in the garden, unholy alliances
forged, one midsummer night, without love.

Inside the reproduction home, they bent over backwards
on neo-Georgian furniture, memorised the statuary,
the brass fittings and sideboard's inner illumination,

every cancellation of surface: the dangerous glass
Deftly inarticulate, they didn't admit her father was gone
until they opened the serving-hatch and all peered through

to see him passed out drunk on the dining-room floor
beneath the rosewood-effect hostess trolley
and a giant painting of thundering breakers

and then she always had to swerve around his empty place
wherever, as if to carefully avoid a porcelain figurine,
a limited edition so rare it had ceased to be visible.

Conch

My grandmother doesn't hear me call; a white mist licks
her skull. She shuffles out to the jungle-yard
to pin a single greying cloth to the drying rack's
sun-dial spines, the dulling weather-vane
where the fading laundry's years have swung and aired.

The piece of washing turns its only two pages
back and forth, re-read by the wind, water veins
mapping the ground, while shadows throw vaguer
and vaguer epitaphs across the sheets snapping in the breeze.
The woman goes inside, and her door shuts again
into the memory I'll always hold of its splintered frieze.

But my real grandmother's sealed thousands of miles away
in her red-brick house deafened with treasure – bone-and-tulle
dancing skirts, dried quills, the family of bells
lined up in ever-decreasing size, their peals subsiding
to a white noise, her shell collection emptying the sea,
vowels bleached on another shore; and from the countless shelves
she's taken her umpteenth book to read in bed, yearning
for me, for the children, her ears burning.

Bargain with the Watchman

There were two extra hooks of a worrying nature.
You'd better say it. We didn't know what we were doing.

The cratered earth, woven with roots, admitted nothing:
only later, when the pegs slid in, the canvas grew taut.

We'd browsed along the Cantal roads like butterflies,
settling lightly in a peaceful upland spot.

But the dogs barked in advance of the enemy,
the farmer riding shotgun on his tractor.

I had to strike a bargain with the watchman:
ten francs, some unwanted perfume and a burgundy kiss.

My shadow's length weighed me down like a lover,
a nightmare pressing: rose-lit arches, confetti or skin.

I was clutching the drooping tail of a pale horse
while you tethered the body, secured the spine.

Useless, I memorised the army-knife's position.
Then we drank their flaming water. Vichy.

Whiteout

If I hold my breath, nothing will fray or melt.
If I hold my breath and rehearse my surrender to stillness

and learn how to smother these curses in white,
I'll hear how the ice breaks off from the soul,
the course of blood turned to water, neat, on the rocks.

Why should I be in love with such dazzling sadness,
the heave of snow right up to the black-coal river
roaming, like a fragile seam through the hills?

The town's jeeps are draped in satin, ruffles bloated
and dragging: the topiary of opulent cradles.

Now. The pendulum swings, after a frozen decade,
cracks the dizzying light. Someone finds purpose
– imagine – starts patiently scraping, scraping away.

The future kick-starts, ploughs Main Street.
I'm free to go, now freedom has me by the throat.

Alex, Tiffany, Meg

rode fast convertibles, rose up like the Furies
blazing scarves and halters in a fire-trail.
The local boys, at first no more than curious,
went mad for the sting in their beautiful tails.

Such kindly girls; they deftly wound my hair
with strange accessories. Naked, like stone,
I bore the slender fingers and thundery stares
as they ripped and ripped away at my bikini-line.

Not ugly, nor evil, they were taken so seriously
their shadows slip beneath each lover, the Fates
re-grouping nightly, featured in the crumpled sheets
or the legacy of silk – my abandoned freight.
Pursued or in pursuit, I find your street
and fly into your bed. Calm this fury, please.

Night-flower

He's drunk again, laid out on the promenade bench,
the sky-line's bright armada bearing down on him.

The river spins their early evening arguments
to smooth black silk. All the world loves a lover.

So a stranger now unzips that rousing dream of her
and in his mouth grows the artificial bloom.

Apocrypha

(for Ann)

We know how hard it is to tell the difference:
to tell if she had not raised her hands in amazed joy
but was standard-bearer for a dangerous river, her life,

snared by the warm wine and the shock of cold current,
a shoe lost, her foothold loosened from the velvet rocks
and long hair stretching like seaweed, from coast to coast.

How to tell? Hands had already erased the shoulders,
her wrist sacrificed to a tongue, one breath unwinding
when the tiny latch in her lungs had slipped with a name.

You could trace it back to a galaxy of her tears
– more empty space than matter, except from a distance.
Now, to accelerate, she hurls out arms, pedals into the dark.

It has long been our custom to disappear in this way,
with a careless spirit, the cables slackened then cut.
A spare thanks to saviours who leave icons on the shore.

Conditional

Given the edge of lilac
nudging the coolish air
– temporary, ripe for admiration –
given the circus of azalea
rounding off the lake
still pitch-black from a weight
of ice, or sheer forgetfulness,

every time, I'd take him in me,
an arrow forcing the point
in an uneasy truce, made for spring,
no angle left considered:
the calculated indecision
of this sort of love
that may be the only possible one.

Grief

I recognise those two full bottles, shared from hand
to hand, relieved of Campari or Martini Rosso
and tipping out a frothy wickedness I'd forgotten,
the summer light stretched to breaking point
across the park. At their age, it's work to drink like that.

Loiterers beneath a Victorian clock stuck at noon,
the eldest craves a more demanding role –
O j'ai mal à la tête. Je me sens malade –
one of elegant degradation. If he only knew how.

Odd, how blonde they are, as if from the same gene-pool:
the final drop of darkness emptied out, from all eight
of those naughty children, cool sentinels, the impostors.

Trepanned

Bad enough, not to have trekked the Himalayas
or smoked a pipe in the back of a Volkswagen bus
with Storm the mechanic, who, with blessings from us
changed the oil and filter en route to enlightenment.
Let's just say you were part of my dimmer days;
I turned the lights down low to cosmic bliss,
laughed at the spirit, in spirits, excited the men.
A corporeal slant. And all I wanted was this:

one little plastic piece of that five-and-dime belief,
a novelty axe to hack at the totems of numbers
on your PC screen. I wanted hand relief –
that is, the gentle touch just before you go under.
Nothing profound, nothing deep. Which is why
I let you drill that Black and Decker into my third eye.

Ursi's Arcadia

The bluebells had greyed,
the foxgloves waiting in the future,
the bracken ascendant in the pause between colour.

Prettiest from this angle:
Walter's thick oak, sideways now
and buttressed with fresh timber to mark his room

in their scowled paddock,
among the exhausted fallen-in seams
from which a Roman mined his life, or death.

The sheep shouldn't complain
being sheared; they never know
they'll be lightened in this heat. An hour to catch them.

She couldn't help or hinder
the flowery tide which surged to the gate,
the unfailing yellow stars of the potentillas

or the climbers sewing her in.
The row of marriage beeches had reached their extreme.
Allow her a modest folly: a Swiss barn – cross-beamed, red-wheeled –

the forest painted inside
so her mournful donkeys could look beyond their winter.
She said: *This is the one creative thing I've done in my life.*

Bye-Bye

I've said it so many times

it's almost comfortable pain:
from the acid ones,
from the short and the cool, the fiery kinds,

the irresistible rewinds.

I could call it life, crying for it or him
to muzak and departure bells,
down angular concourses, a plastic lounge, in rain

I've said it so constantly.

The salt seasons the luggage smell,
the arrival/departure lines,
the engine's whine, a slow farewell

and the kind of goodbye which hasn't a name.

Don't the experts call sublime
how the red wine's bleeding at the rim
denotes its place and age, maturity?

And it was never the break, but the refrain,

coming and going – half lost, half saved –
so you drown repeatedly with each new wave
just to rise to go that way again.

The Buddhas of Bamiyan (19): This was written several months before September 11th, 2001, before the war in Afghanistan. The author grew up in Brooklyn, facing the twin towers, just across the East River.

Helen's Sister (65): In classical mythology, Castor and Pollux were the twin sons of Jupiter and Leda, just as Helen of Troy was the daughter of Zeus and Leda in Greek legend. Castor and Pollux were also the names given by Roman sailors to St Elmo's Fire, or the corposant phenomenon, when the flame effect on the mast of a ship appeared double. This indicated that the worst of the storm was over. A single flame, called Helen's Fire, signified that the worst of the storm was yet to come.

The Old One Two (68): Twins are the ideal control for studies on nature *vs.* nurture. Among recent surprising discoveries is that a far larger percentage of pregnancies than was previously thought began as twins, with one twin lost too early to discern. It is now also believed that identical twins can develop to two separate placentae, while fraternal (or sororal) twins, from two different eggs, can in fact develop within a single placenta. The author is a twin.

Doppelgänger (71): If you spot your Doppelgänger, this is definitely not your lucky day; in fact, according to the story, it is your final day.

The Oxford University Press, in Hospital (81): Oxford University Press, after more than 100 years, closed its poetry list in 1999. Among the reasons cited were loss of money and the desire to concentrate on academic publishing. Robert Bridges, Poet Laureate and Doctor, is commemorated in the Bridges Ward at the Whittington Hospital. He, and other dead poets, continue to be published by said press.

Old Woman Sentimental Song (86): This is not sung to the tune of Tammy Wynette's 'D-I-V-O-R-C-E', but to some other tune.

The Bomb Aria (88): An artist friend, Mark Rowan-Hull, describes a memorable night with some Vietnam Vets, met during his Grand Tour across the United States. Their music of choice was a recorded medley of bombs, each one identified by its timbre and tone. And so they reminisced, recalled the good old days.

Trompe l'œil (103): From 'A Life in the Day' feature in the *Sunday Times*: Nicholas Ridley, then Secretary of State for the Environment, stands before one of his paintings.